HOW

No matter what it is, the important question always is: "How to do it?"

The mind has many marvelous powers—far more than you have ever dreamed of—and humanity has barely begun the wonderful evolutionary journey that will let us tap into them all at will. We grow in our abilities as we do things.

There are many wonderful things you can do. As you do them, you learn more about the innate qualities of mind and spirit, and as you exercise these inner abilities, they will grow in strength—*as will your vision of your mental and spiritual potential.*

In learning *How to Heal with Color*, or See and Read the Aura, or make a Love Charm, or use a Magic Mirror, or many other strange and wonderful things, you are extending—just a little bit—the tremendous gift that lies within, the Life Force itself.

We are born that we may grow, and not to use this gift—not to grow in your perception and understanding of it—is to turn away from the gifts of Life, of Love, of Beauty, of Happiness that are the very reason for Creation.

Learning how to do these things is to open psychic windows to New Worlds of Mind & Spirit. Actually doing these things is to enter into New Worlds. Each of these things that we do is a step forward in accepting responsibility for the worlds that you can shape and influence.

Simple, easy to follow, yet so very rewarding. Following these step-by-step instructions can start you upon high adventure. Gain control over the world around you, and step into *New Worlds of Mind & Spirit.*

About the Author

Ted Andrews is a full-time author, student and teacher in the metaphysical and spiritual fields. He conducts seminars, symposiums, and workshops and lectures throughout the country on many facets of ancient mysticism. Ted works with past-life analysis, auric interpretation, numerology, the Tarot and the Qabala as methods of developing and enhancing inner potential. He is a clairvoyant and certified in spiritual mediumship, basic hypnosis, and acupressure. Ted is also involved in the study and use of herbs as an alternative path. In addition to writing several books, he is a contributing author to various metaphysical magazines.

To Write to the Author

If you wish to contact the author or would like more information about this book, please write to the author in care of Llewellyn Worldwide, and we will forward your request. Both the author and publisher appreciate hearing from you and learning of your enjoyment of this book and how it has helped you. Llewellyn Worldwide cannot guarantee that every letter written to the author can be answered, but all will be forwarded. Please write to:

Ted Andrews
c/o Llewellyn Worldwide
P.O. Box 64383, Dept. L005-2,
St. Paul, MN 55164-0383, U.S.A.

Please enclose a self-addressed, stamped envelope for reply, or $1.00 to cover costs.
If outside the U.S.A., enclose international postal reply coupon.

How to Heal with Color

Ted Andrews

1999
Llewellyn Publications
St. Paul, Minnesota 55164-0383, U.S.A.

FIRST EDITION
Sixth printing, 1999

Cover Painting by Victoria Poyser Lisi
Illustrations by Christopher Wells

Library of Congress Cataloging-in-Publication Data
Andrews, Ted, 1952-
How to heal with color / by Ted Andrews.
p. cm. — (Llewellyn's how to series)
Includes bibliographical references.
ISBN 0-87542-005-2
1. Color—Therapeutic use. 2. Color—Psychological aspects. I. Title. II. Series.
RZ414.6.A63 1992
615.8'31—dc20 92-13176
CIP

Llewellyn Publications
A Division of Llewellyn Worldwide, Ltd.
P.O. Box 64383, St. Paul, MN 55164-0383

Printed in the United States of America

Dedication

To Kodi, Cheyenne, Akasha and Avalon—
The gold within the black and white
Pillars of Balance.

Other Books by Ted Andrews

Animal-Speak
Dream Alchemy
Enchantment of the Faerie Realm
How to Develop and Use Psychic Touch
How to Meet and Work with Spirit Guides
How to See & Read the Aura
How to Uncover Your Past Lives
Imagick
The Healer's Manual
The Magical Name
Magickal Dance
The Occult Christ
The Sacred Power in Your Name
Sacred Sounds
Simplified Magic

CONTENTS

SPECIAL NOTE

The author recognizes that all aspects of the health field, traditional and non-traditional, have their purpose. It is not the intent to give one method credence over another. The purpose is to show the choices we have available. There are many ways of healing the human essence and to participate in restoring balance. We each have our own unique energy system, and we must find the method or combination of methods that works best for us as individuals.

Color therapy is not meant to be a panacea for every health difficulty. Neither is it meant to be a prescription. We cannot prescribe colors like medication. By learning to work with color therapies, you are not practicing medicine. Keep in mind that there are many laws against prescribing and diagnosing.

When we use color therapies, we are simply employing preventative care. We are participating more responsibly and actively in our own health maintenance. The techniques are holistic guidelines only. It is my wish that this work be used to expand your perceptions and provide a different barometer by which you can participate more personally in manifesting your truest health.

Do not accept these things unless your heart whispers so. Remember that there are many philosophies, many methods and many teachers. You do not have to limit yourself to one. Be discriminating and responsible. Use what you learn in the manner that is best for you and all concerned.

1

WORLD OF LIGHT AND COLOR

Everyone has an opinion on colors. Everyone has his or her favorites. Everyone is also affected by colors, often more than is realized. Color is intimately tied into all aspects of our lives. It has even become a significant part of our language. We use colors to describe our physical health, our emotions, attitudes, and even our spiritual experiences. Listen to the conversations that people have. You can't help noticing how frequently color is used as part of our normal vocabulary:

"I'm in the pink today."

"You look at the world through rose-colored glasses."

"He was red with anger."

"His business was in the red last year, but now it is in the black."

"She has the blues today."

"They are all green with envy."

"It was a rich, golden experience."

"He has a yellow streak down his back."

No one is neutral when it comes to colors. There are always some colors we like more than others, and there are some we just do not like at all. Did you ever wonder why this is so? Did you ever wonder what this thing called color is and why it is so important to understand? Does color affect us more than we realize? Can colors be used to alter our physical, emotional, mental and spiritual conditions? And if so, can we all learn to use them to enhance our lives? These questions and more will be answered throughout this text as you learn to experience colors from a new level and learn to heal with them.

To start to answer those questions about colors, let us begin with light. What is light? Light creates color and form. From a scientific point of view, light is electromagnetic energy that is produced by the sun in differing wavelengths. When these light waves bounce off of objects into our eyes, they create the sensation of light. Everything we see is by reflected light. Low frequency light

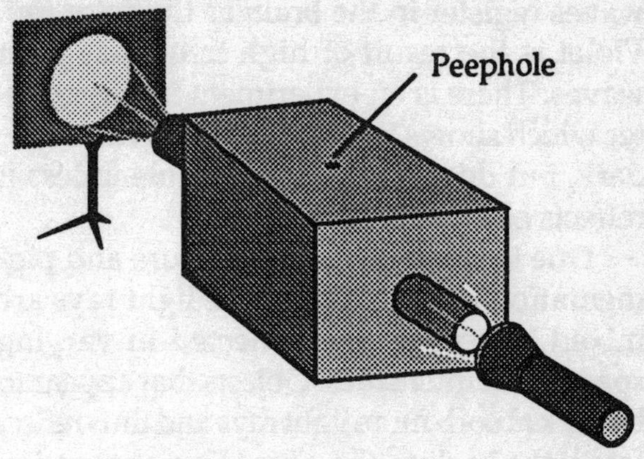

Proving We See by Reflected Light

Paint the inside of a cardboard box a flat black. Make a hole on each end, just large enough to fit half of the tube from a roll of paper towels. Insert the tubes into the box, so that an inch to an inch and a half is inside at each end. Then seal the box tightly so that no light leaks through. Cut a tiny peephole in the top.

Shine a flashlight through one of the tubes. Hold a piece of paper near the other tube to make sure the light is passing through the box. As you do this, look through the peephole. The inside will be completely dark, even though the light is passing through and being reflected on the paper you are holding!

Next allow a little smoke into the box while shining the light through. Now as you look into the peephole, you will see the beam of light passing through. This is because the light is now reflecting off of the particles of smoke.

waves register in the brain as the color red. Violet is the result of high frequency light waves. There is an experiment in this chapter which shows you how light travels in the dark, but does not become visible unless it reflects off of something.

Due to the molecular structure and pigmentation of each object, the light rays are mixed, absorbed and reflected in varying speeds and intensities. Objects that appear to be dark absorb more light rays and thus reflect less light back to the eyes. This absorption creates the illusion of a deeper, darker color. Lighter objects reflect more light, giving the illusion of more brilliance and intensity.

Light waves change speed when they move from one kind of material into another. For example, light travels slower in water than in air. A pencil in a glass of water will appear to be broken and a finger or hand will appear larger when submerged in water. This happens because the light waves are bent as they move from the air to the water. (See "The Speed of Light" illustration.)

Color is also a property of light. When light is broken down (reflected and absorbed) into different wave lengths, we end up with different colors. It is like holding up a prism to the sunlight. It will display a rainbow on

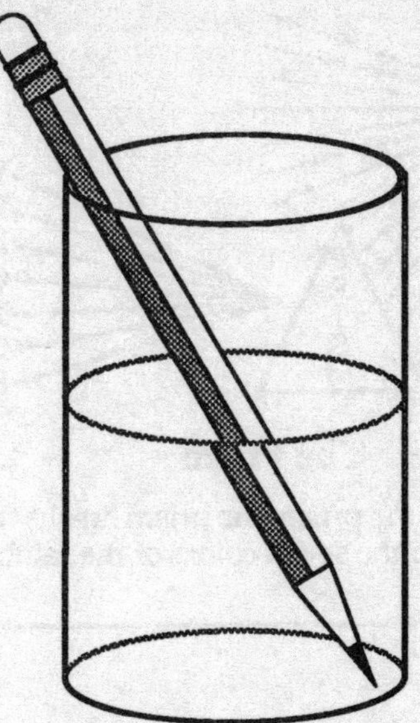

The Speed of Light

Light travels at slower speeds in water than in air. As a result, the reflected light is bent and can create variations and distortions.

---

an opposite surface. (See "The Prism" illustration.) The seven colors of the rainbow are only a small fraction of the entire light spectrum. There are a multitude of shades and variations in each color.

Each color possesses its own absorptive and reflective properties. For example, when

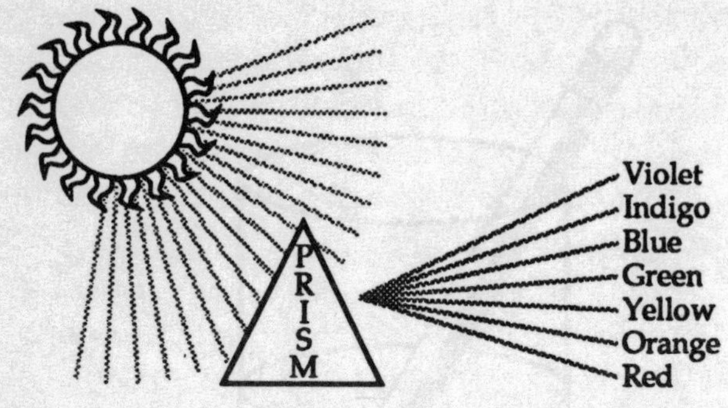

The Prism

As sunlight hits the prism, the prism breaks the light wave down into the seven colors of the rainbow.

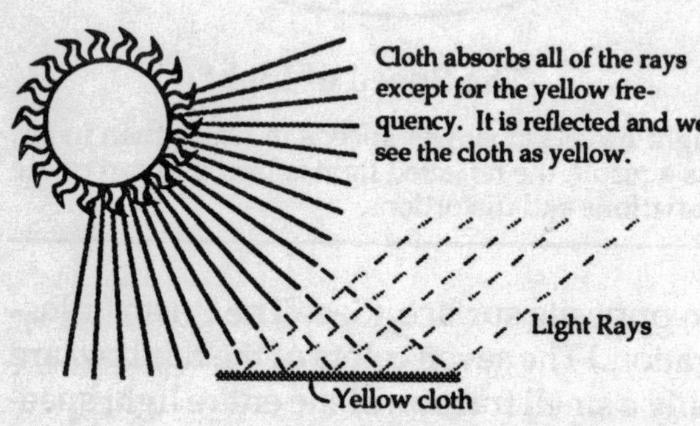

Cloth absorbs all of the rays except for the yellow frequency. It is reflected and we see the cloth as yellow.
Light Rays
Yellow cloth

How We See Color

daylight strikes different colors, all of the light rays are absorbed and reflected according to the object. A yellow cloth will absorb all of the light rays, but it will separate the yellow wave and reflect it back out to the eyes. We see the cloth as yellow.

What does this have to do with healing? Very simply, the different frequencies of light (the colors) will affect different energies of the body. Some colors can more easily affect the higher frequencies of the brain because they have a higher light wave frequency. Other colors can affect the systems or energies of the body (which operates at a slower rate) because they have a lower frequency.

To fully understand this, we must begin to see ourselves as an energy system. Everything in life is formed from vibration. This vibration is the result of the movement of the electrons and protons of every atom in every molecule of every substance in the universe. Vibration exists in objects, in animals, in people, and in the atmosphere surrounding us. The vibrational frequency of animate life is more active, vibrant and variant than inanimate matter, but vibration exists in all things.

The human body is comprised of many energy fields. These energy fields surround, emanate from and can interact with the phys-

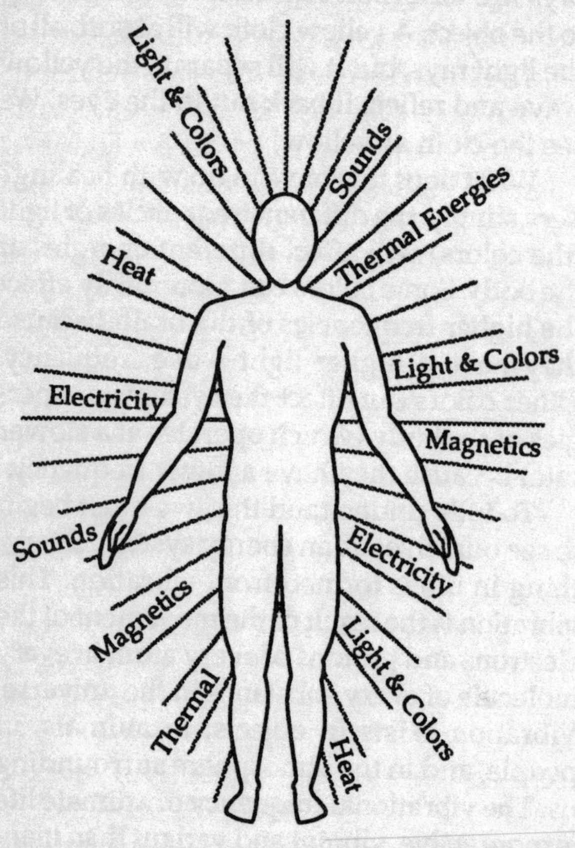

Energy Emanations of the Physical Body

ical body and its various functions. These energy fields include, but are not limited to: light (colors), electricity, heat, sound, magnetism and electromagnetism. They are scientifically measurable. One task of the modern metaphysical scientist is to determine which energies, intensities and combinations are most effective in the healing process.

All of the organs, tissues, and systems within our body are comprised of similarly vibrating atoms. If something irritating (such as an improper food substance) enters the body, it can result in altering the normal vibrational pattern of the body, or in this case the digestive system. At these times, the body needs something to help restore it to its original vibrational pattern. We can use a *vibrational remedy* to temporarily restore balance to that problem area.

Vibrational remedies are subtle energy stimuli which interact with the energy system of the human body to help stabilize physical, emotional, mental and spiritual conditions. By providing the correct focus of energy to the problem area, we can temporarily restore balance to that area. Once balance is restored, we can more effectively rid ourselves of toxins, negativities, and patterns that hinder our life processes. Through vibrational remedies we revive a proper flow of energy. Some of the most effective vibrational remedies are sounds, aromas, flower and gem essences, crystals and stones, thoughts and, of course, COLOR!

2

COLORS AND THEIR EFFECTS

Color is a concentration of a certain light frequency. Color can be stimulating or depressing, constructive or destructive. It can be repellent or attractive. Each color has its own unique effects and can be used for healing and balancing, as well as for stimulating deeper levels of consciousness.

Colors are usually broken down into three categories. First, there are the primary colors of red, yellow, and blue. From a mixture of these three will come most of the other colors. Secondary colors are those formed from combinations of the primary colors. Combinations of the primary colors and the secondary give us tertiary colors. As you learn to combine various colors and their shades, you will develop the ability to adapt your healing techniques to each individual.

The techniques throughout this book will assist you in working with the various colors

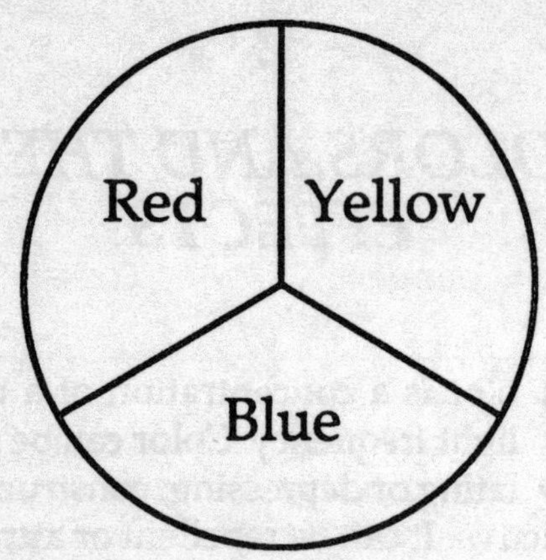

Primary and Secondary Colors

The three primary colors are the foundation from which almost all other colors are derived.

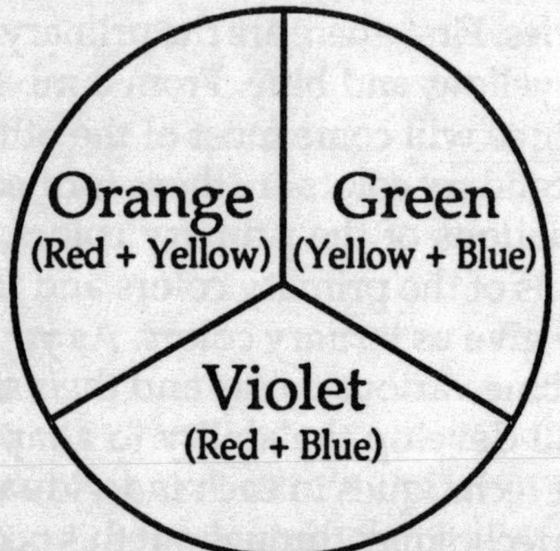

Secondary colors are formed by combining two of the primary colors. Fifty percent of one primary color is added to fifty percent of another to form a new color.

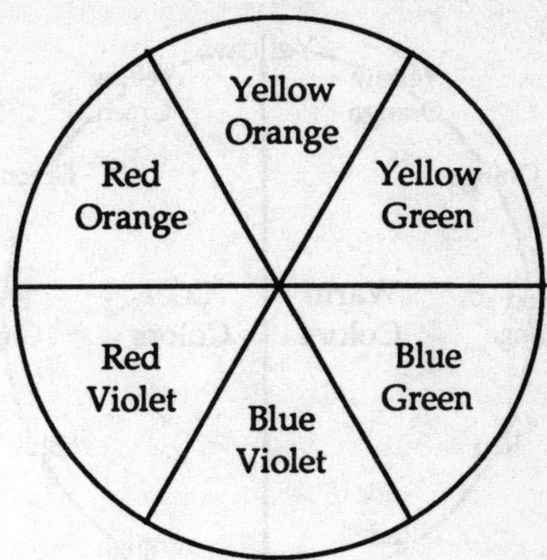

The Tertiary Colors

The tertiary colors are formed by combining a primary color with a secondary color. As you learn to combine different colors and combinations, you begin to form the many shades of color within a particular color's spectrum.

---

and their shades so as to achieve the greatest effect in the healing process. Because each person has his/her own unique energy system, some experimentation is necessary to find the color(s) or shades that are most beneficial for the individual.

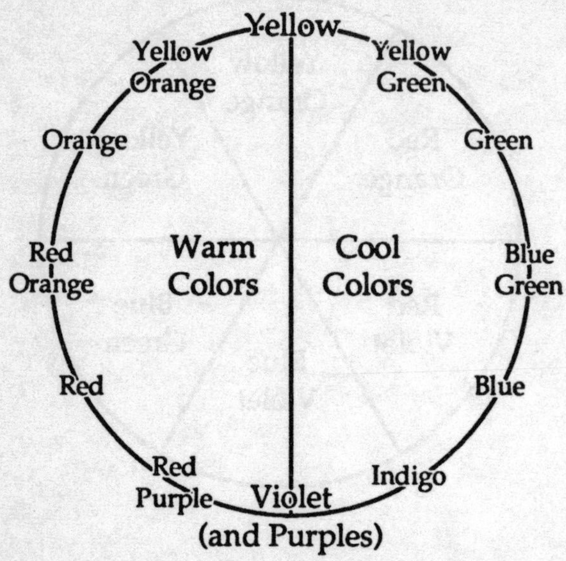

The Colors from a Psychological Perspective

Red is considered to be our psychologically dominant warm color and blue our dominant cool color. The warmer the color, the more red it contains. The cooler the color, the more blue it contains. This is symbolic as well as actual when applied to healing.

Working with colors in healing involves two steps. First, you must understand the individual properties of each color. Second, you must learn specific techniques to project and absorb color. You must become more color sensitive and knowledgeable. The more knowledgeable you become about colors, the easier you will find it to balance and heal with them. At the end of this chapter are several exercises to help you develop color sensitivity. Included is an exercise designed to teach you how to develop your innate ability to project color radiations through your hands. It is the first of many such exercises found throughout this book.

The Meaning of Colors

I have assembled a list of some of the associations of and uses for colors. These are meant to be guidelines. They are not carved in stone. They are characteristics designed to help you begin your work with color therapy. As you work with each individual, you will discover that certain shades are more effective than others, depending upon the person. You may also discover that certain colors may not work for an individual's condition. In cases such as these, a little experimentation and a little intuition will help you discover the best colors to use to obtain results. Remember that each individual has his/her own unique energy system. Thus the colors, the combinations of colors and the manner of their application must always be adapted to the individual.

White—

White contains the entire light spectrum. It is strengthening. It is very cleansing and purifying to the entire energy system of the individual. It can awaken great creativity. When in doubt as to what color to use, you can seldom go wrong with white light. It is also beneficial to begin and end the healing session with white to stabilize the person's energy system and to give it an overall boost. It amplifies the effects of any color with which it is used.

Black—

Black also contains the entire color spectrum. It is also a color that is shrouded in confusion. Many individuals shy away from using black in color therapy and healing, but I have found it beneficial at times. Black is a protective color, and it can be used to ground and calm extremely sensitive individuals. It activates the feminine or magnetic energies of the body, strengthening them. It should be used sparingly, as too much black can cause depression or aggravate such emotional and mental conditions.

Black is most effective when used in conjunction with white, which balances the polarities of the individual, especially in cases where the individual seems to be losing control. It can activate that level of the subconscious which can put life and its craziness into proper perspective. It should never be used by itself, but always in combination with another color.

Red—

Red is a stimulating color. It will energize the base chakra. It warms and it activates. It awakens our physical life force. It can be used for colds, poor circulation and mucus ailments. Red strengthens the physical energy and the will of the individual. It can stimulate deeper passions, such as sex and love, courage, or hatred and revenge. Too much red can overstimulate and aggravate conditions. High blood pressure is an indication of too much red energy within the system. Red can be used to raise the body's temperature and to energize the blood.

Orange—

Orange affects the second chakra center. It is the color of joy and wisdom. It stimulates feelings of sociability. It is tied to our emotional health and to the muscular system of the body. Too much orange affects the nerves and should be balanced with shades of green-blues. Orange can assist in healing conditions of the spleen, pancreas, stomach, intestines, and adrenals. Individuals experiencing emotional paralysis or depression can be helped with this color. It can be used to help re-vitalize the physical body and assist with food assimilation. It makes a good tonic after a bout of illness, for it is good for the eliminative system.

Yellow—

Yellow affects the solar plexus chakra most strongly, and it is stimulating to the mental faculties of the individual. It can be useful for depression. It helps re-awaken an enthusiasm for life. It can be used to awaken greater confidence and optimism. It can be used for digestion problems. It is beneficial to the stomach, the intestines, the bladder and the entire eliminative system of the body. It helps to balance the entire gastrointestinal tract. The golden-yellow shades are healthful to both the body and the mind.

Green—

Green is the most predominant color on the planet. It balances our energies, and it can be used to increase our sensitivity and compassion. It has a calming effect, especially for inflamed conditions of the body. It is soothing to the nervous system. The brighter greens, leaning toward the blue spectrum, are powerful in healing most conditions. Green can be used to awaken greater friendliness, hope, faith and peace. It is restful and re-vitalizing to over-taxed mental conditions.

Green strongly affects the heart chakra, and it is balancing to the autonomic nervous systems. It can be applied beneficially in cardiac conditions, high blood pressure, ulcers, exhaustion, and headaches. It should NEVER be used in cancerous or tumorous conditions or anything of a malignant nature, as green also stimulates growth.

Blue—

Blue is cooling to our system and it is relaxing. It is quieting to our energies, and it has an antiseptic effect as well. It is strengthening and balancing to the respiratory system of the body. It is excellent for high blood pressure and all conditions of the throat. It is effective in easing childhood diseases, along with asthma, chicken pox, jaundice and rheumatism. It is one of the most healing colors for children. It is beneficial to venous conditions of the body. Blue can also be used to awaken intuition and to ease loneliness. Blue is very effective when combined with warmer colors that are in its color range and when combined with colors in the red-orange spectrum. It can also be used to awaken artistic expression and inspiration.

Indigo—

Indigo and the deeper shades of blue are dynamic healing colors on both spiritual and physical levels. This color activates the brow chakra of the body and it is balancing to all conditions associated with it. It is strengthening to the lymph system, the glands, and to the immune system of the body. It is an excellent blood purifier and can assist in detoxifying the body. It is a color that is balancing to the hemispheres of the brain and the nerve synapses between them. It is effective in treating all conditions of the face (including eyes, ears, nose, mouth, and sinuses).

The color indigo also has a sedative effect. You can use the color indigo when you are meditating in order to achieve deeper levels of consciousness. It can awaken devotion and intuition. It can also be used for problems in the lungs and for removing certain obsessions.

Too much indigo can cause depression and a sense of separateness from others.

Violet—

Violet is a color that affects the skeletal system of the body. It is very antiseptic, cleansing, and purifying on physical and spiritual levels. It helps balance the physical and the spiritual energies. Violet is good to use for cancerous conditions of the body. Arthritis can be eased by violet light that leans more toward the blue shades. Violet is also strengthening to the body's ability to assimilate and use minerals. Violet can be used to stimulate inspiration and humility. Violet assists in stimulating dream activity as well. In meditation, violet can help open us to our past lives.

Pink—

Pink can be used to awaken compassion, love, and purity. It eases conditions of anger and feelings of neglect. It helps stimulate the thymus gland and the immune system of the body. It can be used in meditation to discern greater truths. Pink is comforting to the emotional energies of the individual.

Lemon—

Lemon is vitalizing and stimulating to the brain. It contains a shade of green within its spectrum, and this works as a cleanser.

Lemon assists in bringing toxins to the surface so they can be cleaned out. Lemon is also good for tissue and bones.

Gold—

Gold is a powerful stimulant to the immune system of the body. It helps awaken the individual's own healing energies to assist the body in restoring homeostasis. It can also awaken enthusiasm.

Royal Blue—

This color is very antiseptic and it helps the body assimilate oxygen. It can clear the foggy mind and is an aid to negative physical conditions that affect the brain.

Aqua—

Aqua is cooling to the system. It can be beneficial in easing feverish conditions and for balancing out the systems of the body. It can be used to cool and ease inflammations.

Turquoise—

Turquoise is cooling to the system. It combines the beneficial effects of blue and green, vitalizing the system and purifying as well. It is effective in skin conditions. It is also effective for acute pain and earaches.

Purple—

Purple is purifying to the system, but because of its high vibration, it should be used sparingly. Too much purple can create or aggravate depression. It can be used to stimulate venous activity in the body. It can also be used for headaches. The red-purple range is beneficial for balancing polarities of the body. The blue-purple range can often be used effectively to shrink things (as in the case of tumors) and to cool the skin, easing inflammation.

Silver—

Silver and some grays can be used to amplify the effects of other colors, much in the manner of white. Silver is effective in meditations used to discover the metaphysical source of an illness or dis-ease. Unless we discover the source, the likelihood of its reoccurrence is high. It can also be used to help an individual discover and apply their own creative imagination. It activates innate intuition.

Brown—

Brown is also a color that can be used in healing. It is especially effective for emotional and mental conditions. Brown can help awaken common sense and discrimination. It can help bring an individual "back down to earth." It is effective for that spacy feeling.

Common Ailments and Beneficial Colors

This list is only a guideline. It is NOT prescriptive. It is a set of suggestions to help you find a starting point in working with color therapy. It is not designed to replace traditional medicine, rather it is to provide a means by which you can participate more personally in your own healing process. Use it as such, so that you can develop your own system of color application. Find what works for you. You may need to apply different colors with different intensities. Often, experimentation is the only way we have of discovering what works for the individual.

Begin all color treatments with white and end them with white. This amplifies the treatment's effect and it serves to keep the color treatments from aggravating a condition. It provides balance. Remember that the red spectrum affects the physical, and is stimulating and warming. Blues are cooling and cleansing, affecting the spiritual energies. The yellow shades affect the mental energies and serve as a bridge between the physical and the spiritual.

The three together—reds, blues and yellows—provide opportunities for healing body, spirit, and mind.

Conditions & Corresponding Colors

Condition	Beneficial Colors
Abdominal Cramps	Yellow, Lemon
Abscesses	Blue, Blue-Violet
Aches (ear)	Turquoise
Aches (head)	Blue, Green
Aches (muscles)	Pastel Orange
Aches (tooth)	Blue, Blue-Violet
Acne	Red, Red-Violet
AIDS	Red, Indigo, and Violet, followed by Pink and Gold
Alcoholism	Indigo and Yellow
Allergies	Indigo and Soft Orange
Alzheimer's disease	Royal Blue; Blue-Purple followed by Yellow
Anemia	Red
Anxieties	Light Blue and Green
Appetite (excessive)	Indigo
Appetite (loss)	Yellow, Lemon
Arthritis	Violet, Blue-Violet and Red-Violet
Asthma	Blue and Orange

Conditions & Corresponding Colors (Cont.)

Condition	Beneficial Colors
Bladder	Yellow-Orange
Bleeding	Blue-Green
Blisters	Powder or Ice Blue
Blood Pressure (high)	Blue, Green
Blood Pressure (low)	Red, Red-Orange
Bones	Violet, Lemon
Bowels	Yellow-Orange
Breast	Pink, Red-Violet
Bronchitis	Blue, Blue-Green, Turquoise
Burping	Yellow; Lemon
Burns	Blue; Blue-Green
Cancer	Blue; Blue-Violet followed by Pink
Colds	Reds
Diabetes	Violet
Eczema	Lemon
Epilepsy	Turquoise, Deep Blues
Eyes	Indigo, Royal Blue
Fevers	Blue
Growths	Violet, Blue-Violet
Hay Fever	Red-Orange
Heart Problems	Green and Pink

Condition	Beneficial Colors
Hemorrhoids	Deep Blue
Indigestion	Yellow, Lemon
Infection	Violet
Inflammation	Blue
Influenza	Deep Blue, Turquoise, Violet
Kidneys	Yellow, Yellow-Orange
Leukemia	Violet
Liver	Blue and Yellow combinations
Menstrual Problems	Soft Reds and Blue-Green combinations
Nausea	Ice Blue
Nerves	Green, Blue-Greens
Parkinson's	Indigo
Pneumonia	Red and Red-Orange, combined with Indigo
Rash	Lemon and Turquoise
Skin Problems	Lemon, Blue-Violet
Swelling	Pale and Ice Blues
Ulcers	Green

3

DEVELOPING COLOR SENSITIVITY

We are all sensitive to color. We know which colors we like. We also know which colors we dislike. We can tell, even if we can't define why, when a color is not right for someone. Color and light do affect us. The more sensitive we can become to color and its effects, the more we can use it to our benefit.

One of the easiest ways of developing greater color sensitivity and knowledge is through color flashcards. Simply get a set of 3 x 5 index cards. On one side of the card, list the various attributes of a specific color. On the opposite side, use markers, or crayons to color it appropriately. Have one card for every color. Begin with the seven colors of the rainbow.

Next, relax your mind. Perform a progressive relaxation or some rhythmic breathing. Take a moment or two to study the cards one at a time. Focus on the color, and then read the characteristics to yourself. Go through all of the colors several times.

The next step is to become sensitive to how the colors feel. Our hands have the capability of sensing energy changes and differences. We have all experienced some aspects of this. When we touch someone or shake their hand, we get impressions about that person. Our hands—our sense of touch—help us to attune to that individual's energy. We can apply this ability to developing color sensitivity.

With eyes closed, shuffle and mix the colored cards. Make sure that the colored surface of your index cards are facing up. Pull one from the set, and hold your hand over it. Stay relaxed. Allow your hand to do the sensing. Begin by trying to determine if it has a warm feel or a cool feel. This lets you know whether it is in the red (warm) spectrum or the blue (cool) spectrum.

What else do you feel or sense as you hold your hand over the color? Do you think you know what color it may be? Is there any kind of tingling? Do you notice anything in any particular part of your body? Pay attention to every impression—no matter how odd it may seem. These little details will eventually help you in becoming more knowledgeable about the color and its possible effects and applications.

With practice, you will develop the ability to identify the color by its feel. You are working with subtle vibrational energies. You are working to develop your sensitivity to those subtle energy fields surrounding you. With practice, you will not only be able to sense colors with your hands, you will also be able to project color energies with them.

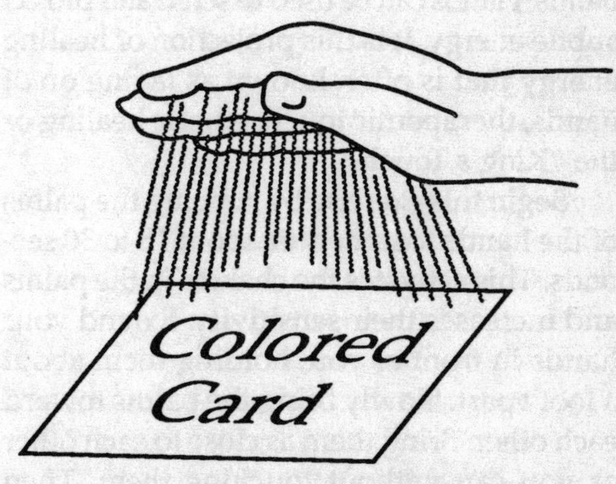

Developing a Sensitivity to Color Through Touch

Color Therapy Through Touch

In this exercise we learn that we can project energies using thought and our own hands. An old occult axiom teaches that all energy follows thought. Where we put our thoughts, that is where our energy goes. If we focus on a color, the energy emanations from the body begin to change to a frequency that resonates with that particular color.

Energy emanates more strongly from the hands than from other parts of the body. Minor chakra points are in the palms of the hands. Hands can be used to sense and project subtle energy. It is this projection of healing energy that is often known as laying on of hands, therapeutic touch, etheric healing or the "King's Touch."

Begin this exercise by rubbing the palms of the hands together for about 15 to 30 seconds. This activates the chakras in the palms and increases their sensitivity. Extend your hands in front of you, holding them about a foot apart. Slowly bring the palms toward each other. Bring them as close to each other as you can without touching them. Then draw them slowly apart to about six inches, and repeat this in and out movement. Keep your movements slow and steady.

As you perform this exercise, pay attention to what you feel or sense. You may feel warmth or coolness. You may experience a feeling of pressure building up. It may seem as if the space between the hands is thickening. There may be a sense of tickling or of pressure. you may even experience a pulsating feeling.

Color Therapy Through Touch

The in and out movement of the hands causes the energy surrounding them and emanating from them to accumulate, making it more perceptible to us.

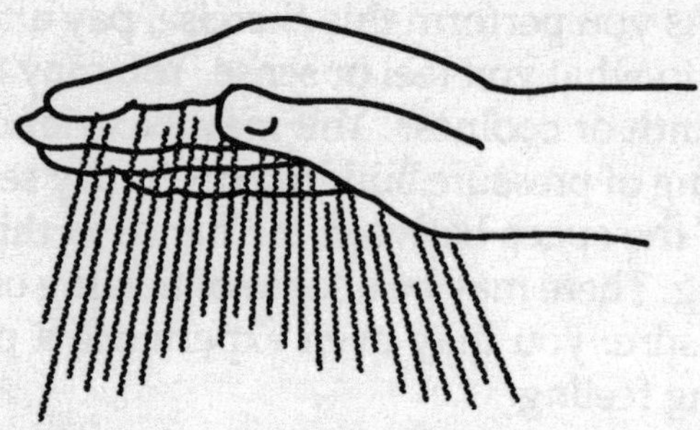

With practice, we can control the intensity and the flow of this energy through our hands by focusing the mind on a specific color.

Take a few minutes to try and define what you are feeling. Do not worry whether you are imagining it or not. Do not worry that it may feel different from how others may experience it. It is important to begin to define it for yourself. This exercise develops concentration, and it helps to confirm that our energy field does not stop at skin level. It also helps you to define your own energy radiations.

The next step is to learn that you can control the intensity of the energy radiations from your hands. This can be most easily accomplished with an everyday outdoor thermometer. Begin by making yourself comfortable and relaxed. Again, rub the palms of your hands together briskly to activate the chakras in them. Take the thermometer and place it between your hands. You may either hold it in your hands or stand it up so that your hands are two to three inches from either side of it.

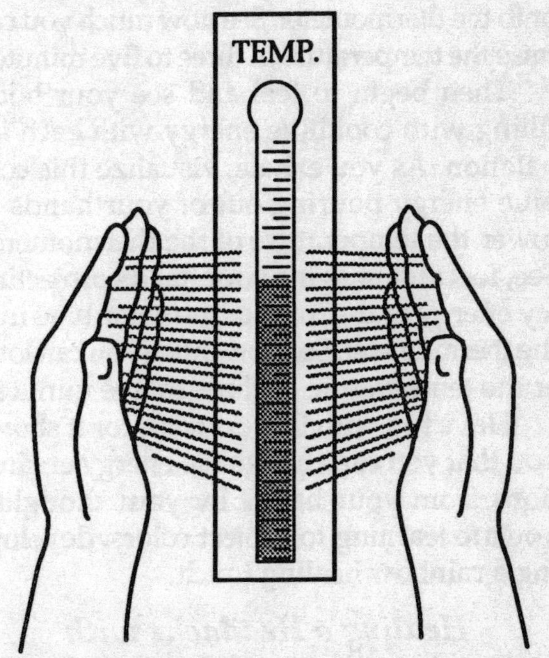

Changing the Temperature

As we learn to radiate energy through our hands, we can change temperature by color—red to warm something, blue to cool it.

Begin to do some slow, rhythmic breathing. As you breathe in slowly, see and feel your body filling with bright, warm red energy. As you exhale, see and feel this bright, warm red energy pouring out of your hands toward the thermometer. Visualize, sense, and project heat—red heat—from your hands onto the thermometer. See how much you can raise the temperature in three to five minutes.

Then begin to feel and see your body filling with cool blue energy with each inhalation. As you exhale, visualize this cool blue energy pouring out of your hands to lower the temperature of the thermometer. See, feel and imagine your hands projecting icy energy in the form of the color blue into the thermometer. See how much you can lower the temperature in three to five minutes.

Have fun with this exercise, for it shows you that you can change the energy emanations from your hands by your thoughts. You are learning to project colors, developing a rainbow healing touch.

Healing a Headache with a Touch of Color

One of the most common ailments is the headache. It is also one of the simplest to eliminate through color. Most headaches are the result of an overstimulation of the brow or crown chakra. It is almost as if they become slightly inflamed. Cooling those centers down serves to alleviate the problem.

We learned in the previous exercise that we can project energy through our hands at a frequency associated with the color upon which we are focusing. We simply apply this to the headache. We will project a soft, cool blue or a blue-green combination for most headaches. For deeper seated pains, such as in the case of migraines, projecting an indigo color is beneficial.

Take a few moments to relax yourself. Begin some rhythmic breathing. As you breathe in, feel the blue energy gathering and building in the body and moving toward the hands, ready to be projected outward.

Have the person with the headache sit down in front of you. Instruct them to just close their eyes and relax. Place your hands two to three inches from the front and the back of the individual's head. (See the illustration "Healing a Headache with Color.") If you wish, you can lay your hands directly on the person's head. Continue your breathing. As you exhale, see and feel this cool blue energy filling the head of the person, balancing, calming and soothing the pain.

Picture the blue as a colored aspirin if it helps. You may wish to move the hands to the sides of the head, where the temples are located. Noticeable results usually occur in less than five minutes.

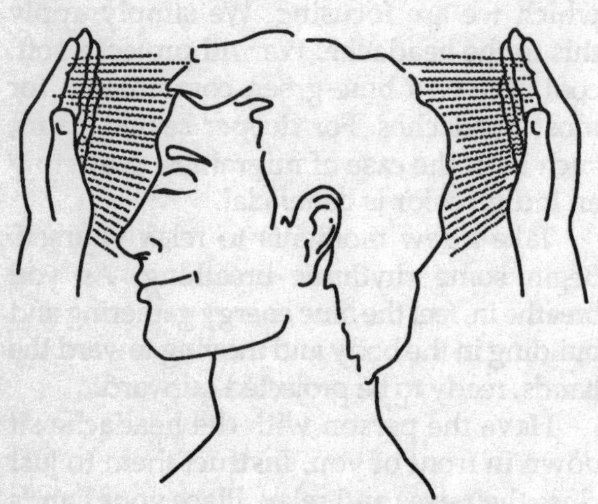

Healing a Headache with Color

All energy follows thought. As we concentrate the mind on a particular color, that signal is sent to the energy which is being projected from the hands. The color upon which we focus determines the vibration of that projection. We can use our hands to heal or alleviate conditions through simple touch.

4

COLOR THERAPY FOR THE CHAKRAS

Because the human body is an energy system, we can use different energy forms to interact with the functions of that system. Understanding the human chakra system is the key to understanding how to use color as a part of the healing process. The word "chakra" comes from the Sanskrit, and it means wheel.

Chakras are the primary mediators of all energy coming into and radiating out from the body. They mediate the impulses of our energy system. Although not part of the physical body, they link the subtle energy fields surrounding the body to the activities of the body itself. Although often thought of as metaphysical "mumbo jumbo," modern science has shown that in the areas of the body where chakras are traditionally located, the electromagnetic emanations are higher.

The chakras help the body distribute energy for its various physical, emotional, mental and spiritual functions. They are connected to the functions of the physical body primarily through the endocrine glands and spinal system. They mediate energy inside and outside of the body through the various spinal contacts. This energy is distributed throughout the body by means of the nerve pathways and the circulatory system. In this way, all of the organs, tissues and cells receive the vibrational energy accordingly.

One of the most effective means of restoring balance is through the use of color. Individual chakras and the related organs and systems in the body will respond to specific colors. If there is an imbalance, we can use colors or combinations of colors to restore homeostasis (balance) to the chakra and thus to those systems and energies of the body mediated by that chakra. The color vibrations interact with the electromagnetic emanations of the body. They are transmitted to the vertebrae of the spine. The vertebrae transfers the color frequencies along the nerve pathways to the organs and systems of the body, restoring balance. This applies also to those emotional and mental imbalances that can cause or aggravate the physical problems.

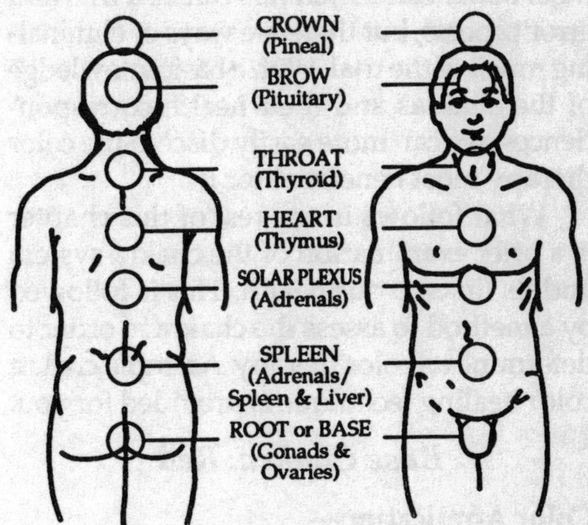

The Chakra System

The chakras help distribute energy for our physical, emotional, mental and spiritual functions. The seven major chakras are points of greater electromagnetic activity within the auric field. The hands and feet are other points of great activity. The subtle auric energies are more easily detectable around them.

The most confusing aspect of working with colors is deciding which color(s) will be most beneficial. Often this can be a trial and error process, but there are ways of eliminating much of the trial. With a basic knowledge of the chakras and their health correspondences, we can more easily discern the color therapy most beneficial for us.

What follows in the rest of this chapter is a brief examination of the chakra system and its links to our health. This is followed by a method to assess the chakra in order to determine its color therapy. A simple chakra color healing technique is provided for you.

Base Chakra: Red

Color Application—

If underactive, use red; if overactive, use green followed by a small dose of red.

Physical Functions—

This chakra is located in the area of the coccyx at the base of the spine. It is tied to the functions of the circulatory system, reproductive system and the functions of the lower extremities. It is the center for our basic life force. It influences the testicles and ovaries, the legs, feet, and pelvic area of the body.

Metaphysical Functions—

This is a center tied to that level of consciousness which controls our life-promoting energies. Stimulated properly, it can awaken awareness of past life talents and ease fears.

Emotional/Mental Attitudes Causing or Reflecting Dysfunction—

Overactive Base Chakra:

Physically aggressive, belligerent, impulsive, inability to recognize limits, obsessively sexual, hyperactive, reckless.

Underactive Base Chakra:

Manipulative, overly cautious, power conscious, possessive, needing approval, craving excitement and change but refusing to act upon it, overly tired, no energy to do what you want. Reactiveness; aggression; belligerence; manipulative.

Spleen Chakra: Orange

Color Application—

If underactive apply orange; if overactive use blue followed by a small dose of orange.

Physical Functions—

This center is partially tied to the function of the adrenal glands. It is also a major influence on the reproductive system and the entire muscular system. It affects the eliminative system of the body, the activities of the spleen, bladder, pancreas, and kidneys. It is a major center for detoxifying the body.

Metaphysical Functions—

This center influences sensation and emotion, desire, pleasure and sexuality. It is linked to the consciousness of creativity. It controls many personality functions. It can be stimulated with color to open communication with energies and beings upon the astral plane of life.

Emotional/Mental Attitudes Causing or Reflecting Dysfunction—

Overactive Spleen Chakra:

Selfish, arrogant, lustful, overly proud or conceited; high-strung emotionally, constant power-seeking.

Underactive Base Chakra:

Mistrustful of others, introverted, unable to show emotions, worrying what others think, anti-social, follows the crowd.

Solar Plexus Chakra: Yellow

Color Application—

If underactive, use yellow; if overactive, use violet or purple, with a small dose of yellow.

Physical Functions—

This chakra is tied to the solar plexus area of the body. This includes the digestive system, the adrenals, the stomach, the liver and the gall bladder. It assists the body in assimilation of nutrients. It is also tied to the functions of the left hemisphere of the brain. Many crippling diseases, ulcers, intestinal problems and psychosomatic diseases are eased by working with this center.

Metaphysical Functions—

This center is tied to the level of consciousness which can make us clairsentient —the ability to sense the feelings and emotions of others. It is a center of empathy and general psychic impressions. When stimulated, it opens awareness of the talents and capacities of other souls. It helps attune us to the elements of nature.

Emotional/Mental Attitudes Causing or Reflecting Dysfunction—

Overactive Solar Plexus Chakra:

Judgmental and critical, mentally bullying, absolutist in attitude, always planning and never manifesting, stubborn, needing constant change/variety.

Underactive Solar Plexus Chakra:

Feeling deprived of recognition, aloof, feeling isolated, afraid to learn the new, psychosomatic problems.

Heart Chakra: Green

Color Application—

If underactive, use green; if overactive, use green, followed by pink or soft reds.

Physical Functions—

This center is influential in the function of the thymus gland and the entire immune system of the body. It is tied to the heart and the pulmonary activities, along with the circulatory system. It affects the assimilation of nutrients. It has a powerful influence on childhood diseases and the developing of a strong immune system from them. It also has ties to activities of tissue regeneration.

Metaphysical Functions—

This center mediates and balances the activities of the other chakras. If it is out of balance, there is likely to be imbalance in the others. It is tied to that level of our consciousness which awakens higher compassion and our innate healing abilities. If stimulated properly with color, it can open an ability to see the deeper forces in plants and animals, along with a knowledge of the sentiments and true dispositions of others.

Emotional/Mental Attitudes Causing or Reflecting Dysfunction—

Overactive Heart Chakra:

Angry, jealous, blaming others, miserly and stingy, overconfident, allowing oneself to be walked on and taken advantage of.

Underactive Heart Chakra:

Needing constant confirmation of self worth, uncertain, unable to enforce will, possessive, self-doubting, feeling unloved, lacking compassion.

Throat Chakra: Blue

Color Application—

If underactive, use blue; if overactive, use orange followed by a small dose of blue.

Physical Functions—

The throat chakra is tied to the functions of the throat, esophagus, mouth, teeth, the thyroid, and the parathyroid glands. It strongly affects the respiratory system, the functions of the bronchia, and the entire vocal apparatus.

Metaphysical Functions—

This chakra is tied to the functions of the right hemisphere of the brain and the creative functions of the mind. It can be stimulated with color to awaken clairaudience and to assist us in manifesting greater abundance. It can be stimulated so as to survey the thoughts of others (telepathy), and it can awaken that level of consciousness which has insight into the true laws of natural phenomena.

Emotional/Mental Attitudes Causing or Reflecting Dysfunction—

Overactive Throat Chakra:

Domineering, dogmatic, fanatical, over-reacting, speaks negatively/harshly, clings to tradition, hyperactive.

Underactive Throat Chakra:

Surrenders to others, resists change, melancholy, slow to respond, stubborn.

Brow Chakra: Indigo

Color Application—

If underactive, use indigo; if overactive, use soft orange or peach followed by a small dose of indigo.

Physical Functions—

The brow center influences the functions of the pituitary and the entire endocrine system. It also has links to the immune system. It affects the synapses of the brain, and it is key to balanced operation of the hemispheres of the brain. It affects the sinuses, eyes, ears, and the face in general.

Metaphysical Functions—

This is the center affecting higher clairvoyance and the entire magnetism of the body (the feminine aspects of our energies). It is linked to that level of the subconscious mind which controls intuitive perceptions, creative imagination and visualization.

Emotional/Mental Attitudes Causing or Reflecting Dysfunction—

Overactive Brow Chakra:

Worrying, fearful, oversensitive, impatient, belittling the behaviors of others, "spaced out."

Underactive Brow Chakra—:
Doubting, envious of other's talents, forgetful, superstitious, fearful, worrying.

Crown Chakra: Violet

Color Application—

If underactive, use violet; if overactive, use yellow followed by a small dose of violet.

Physical Functions—

This center affects the functions of the entire nervous system and the entire skeletal system of the body. It influences the pineal gland, all nerve pathways, and the electrical synapses within the body. It is linked to the proper function of the medulla oblongata.

Metaphysical Functions—

This chakra is a link to that level of the subconscious mind which has ties to our most spiritual essence. It is a center which helps to align us with the higher forces of the universe, and it has a powerful influence in the purification of our subtle bodies of energy. This center is a link to past lives and their effects upon us in the present.

Emotional/Mental Attitudes Causing or Reflecting Dysfunction—

Overactive Crown Chakra:

Intensely erotic imagination, needing to feel popular and indispensable, needing sympathy.

Underactive Crown Chakra:

Feeling misunderstood, shame, self-denial, negative self-image, lacking tenderness.

Chakra Assessment

The ancient masters taught their students to be ever watchful.This meant paying attention to the various emotions and attitudes that they were exposed to or experienced throughout the day. As they did this, they could then determine which chakra center(s) was most likely to be unbalanced. They would then take extra care to balance those centers at the end of the day. In this manner, the imbalance did not have a chance to accumulate, ultimately causing or aggravating a physical problem. We can do the same thing.

We have just examined the chakra system of the body. We now understand how the various physical systems and organs of the body are affected by the chakras and how emotional and mental attitudes can aggravate or create dysfunction in the chakras and their corresponding physical elements. We also listed the primary colors for the chakras.

With that knowledge behind us, we are now ready to do the chakra assessment technique. In this assessment technique, we examine the problem area and determine which chakra is most likely to be unbalanced. Usually, the chakra associated with a particular problem will be overactive or underactive.

As you know, there are specific colors that are useful to balance chakras. Those colors and conditions were already listed earlier in this book. We can use these specific colors to help balance the chakra, and thus we ease the physical, emotional, mental or even spiritual problem.

An underactive chakra is usually one in which the energy is congested. In a congested chakra, the energy does not flow freely through the chakra and its physical systems. A congested base chakra, for example, may reflect itself in physical conditions such as tiredness, anemia, etc. Keep in mind that this is the center for our basic life force. If it is congested or underactive, we just do not have

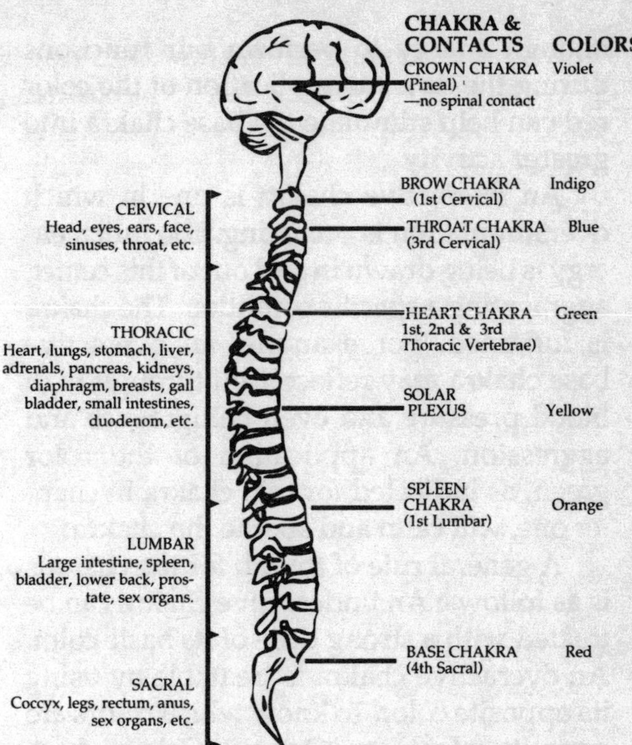

Spinal Contacts of the Chakras

Color vibrations enter through the chakras. They balance the chakras and are transmitted to the vertebrae of the spine. The vertebrae transfer these along the nerve pathways to the various organs and systems to which they are linked. Balance is restored.

enough energy to perform our functions during the day. An application of the color red can help stimulate the base chakra into greater activity.

An overactive chakra is one in which overstimulation is occurring. Too much energy is being drawn in and out of this center, aggravating a specific condition. The chakra is inflamed. For example, an overactive base chakra may reflect itself through high blood pressure and even belligerence and aggression. An application of the color green, as indicated for that chakra in chapter one, will calm and soothe the chakra.

A general rule of thumb for the chakras is as follows: An underactive chakra can be treated with a strong dose of its basic color. An overactive chakra is treatable by using its opposite color. To know which colors are opposite, refer to the "Opposite Colors" chart. If in doubt, apply varying amounts of both colors to the chakra center. The opposite colors balance each other.

Simply follow these basic steps in this process:

1. Determine which chakra(s) are most likely out of balance. The physical condition, the various emotional and mental attitudes,

will assist you in pinpointing the center. Use the charts in chapter one to assist you.

2. Determine if the chakra is overactive or underactive. If underactive, the energy and operation of physical systems involved will seem congested and slow. Overactive is usually reflected by inflammation, agitation and hypersensitivity.

3. Apply the color therapy. You can use the methods described at the end of this chapter or any combination of methods described throughout the book. The length of the color treatment will vary. In many cases you will have to use your intuition. Five to ten minutes per color is effective. You may wish to use the techniques described in the next chapter to assist you in determining the length of the treatment.

4. After applying the color for the specific chakra, it is beneficial to follow it with a general balancing of all seven chakra centers. Do a quick ten to fifteen second color treatment for each chakra center, from the base to the crown. This further stabilizes your system.

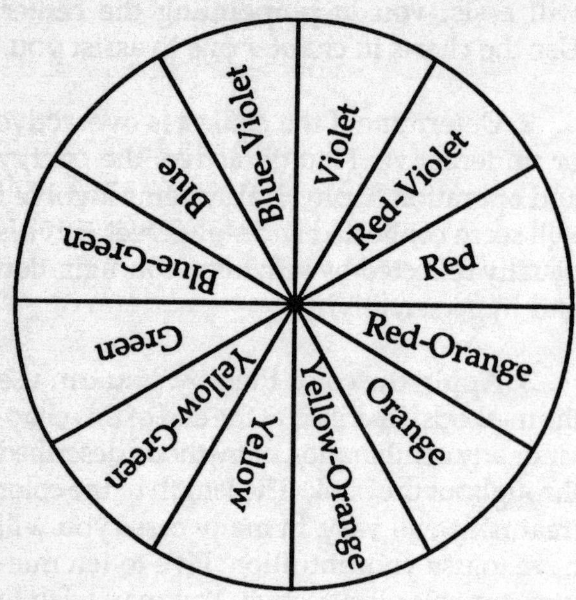

The Opposite Colors Chart

When we determine that a chakra is unbalanced, we then must decide whether it is overactive or underactive. If it is underactive, we simply apply the basic color of that chakra center. If it is an overactive chakra, we apply its opposite color to restore balance to it.

Color Therapy for the Chakras

We can use color therapy to balance ourselves everyday. In this way, we keep ourselves stronger, more balanced and more vibrant. Any of the color application methods throughout the book can be used for this daily balancing. One of the easiest ways this can be accomplished is with simple color swatches that can be bought for two to three dollars at any fabric store. Most fabric stores sell felt or other cloth squares for about 20 cents a piece. They can be found in all of the colors of the rainbow as well as in other shades. Once you have purchased them, you can begin your quick daily chakra color balancing.

1. Make sure that you will be undisturbed for about 10 to 15 minutes. It will rarely take any longer. Make sure the phone is off the hook, etc.

2. Lie down on your back on the floor or on your bed. Have your seven cloth swatches with you (red, orange, yellow, green, blue, indigo and violet).

3. Close your eyes and relax. Take several deep breaths. As you begin to relax, look back over the day, in reverse order. Start with the moment you laid down and look back over the events of the day—all the way back to when you first got out of bed. (When we look at the day in reverse order, we concentrate more, and we are less likely to skip over events and situations.)

4. Note the major emotions and attitudes that you experienced and were exposed to. What chakras were most likely to have been affected by them? Use the information on the chakras from the previous pages to assist you.

5. When you have completed your evaluation, take the color swatches for those chakras you have just identified, and lay them on the part of your body associated with that chakra. (See the illustration "Chakra Color Therapy.")

6. As you lie there with the color swatches upon your chakra points, visualize the colors being absorbed and drawn into your body. Know that as you lie there the chakras are balanced by the color. Take several deep

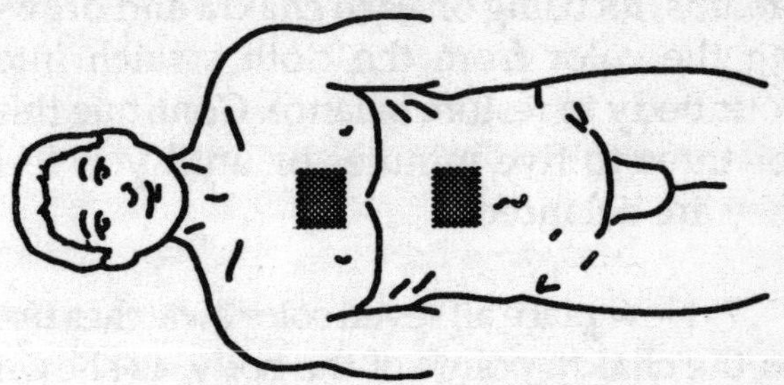

Chakra Color Therapy

Begin by laying the colored cloth pieces upon those chakras you determined were most likely to be unbalanced.

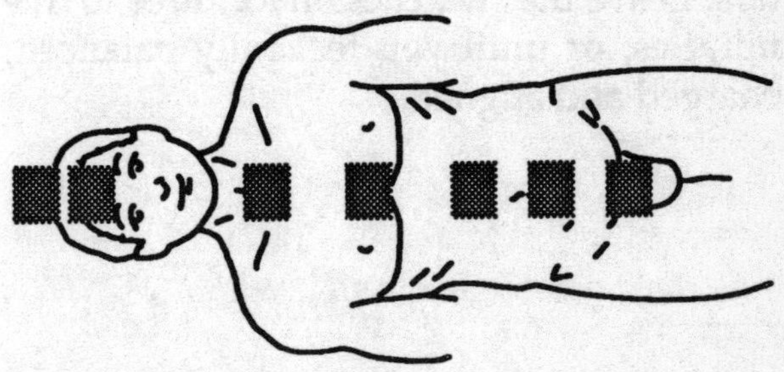

Next, lay the colored cloth swatches on each of the seven major chakras. Make sure you use the appropriate color for each center. Then just allow your body to absorb the energy for several minutes.

breaths, focusing on each chakra and drawing the color from the cloth swatch into your body to restore balance. Continue this for three to five minutes or until you feel they are balanced.

7. Now place all seven color swatches upon the chakra points of the body, as shown in the illustration. Breathe deeply and allow your body to absorb the rainbow energies. Know that they are aligning and strengthening. Feel yourself balancing. Know that all of the physiological aspects of your body are being balanced and healed as you absorb these colors through your chakra centers. Leave the swatches on for three to five minutes, or until you feel fully balanced, charged and aligned.

5

DETERMINING THE COLORS NEEDED

The most confusing aspect of working with colors is deciding which color(s) will be the most beneficial. Often this can be a trial and error process, but there are ways of eliminating much of the trial.

We examined one such method in the last chapter, performing a chakra assessment by taking note of different conditions (physical or otherwise) that were affecting the person at the time. We will explore two more methods of color determination in this chapter. You do not have to use these techniques independently. All of these methods can be used separately or in combination. In all three methods, we are simply working to identify the subtle influences affecting us. It is in these ways that we can more specifically determine the appropriate color therapy which will be the most beneficial for us.

Determining Color Therapy Through Radiesthesia

Radiesthesia is a method of dowsing or divining to determine energy radiation. This is how it works: Our nervous system responds to subtle energies. Often, we don't recognize these subtle energies are there. Radiesthesia involves using a tool to translate those unrecognized energies into something more tangible. The two most common tools of radiesthesia are the dowsing rod and the pendulum.

Any tool of radiesthesia has capabilities that go beyond mere healing. You can use radiesthesia tools to facilitate access to the subconscious mind. They can be used to awaken and activate your own psychic and intuitive feelings, to uncover past lives, to establish links with higher levels of knowledge, and to determine dream meanings. The pendulum and the dowsing rod are tools I recommend for all who are involved in metaphysics because they have so many applications.

The pendulum is particularly effective in helping us to determine appropriate colors (and their combinations) for therapy. The pendulum is a tool for communicating with the subconscious mind. Our subconscious is aware of every energy inside or outside of the body. Through the pendulum, we expand our conscious perception by tapping into the subconscious bank of knowledge.

The pendulum gives no answer itself. The subconscious mind communicates to us through the nervous system. The nervous system translates the communication to an electrical signal and impulse which causes the pendulum to move. The swinging of the pendulum is an ideomotor response. It is caused by involuntary muscle action stimulated by the subconscious mind through the sympathetic nervous system of the body.

Pendulums can be made from simple objects found around the home. Just make sure that the object used as a weight is heavy enough to swing, and that it is able to hang freely. There are four types of common pendulums. (See the illustration "Common Types of Pendulums.")

The first step to using a pendulum is to get the feel of it. Take a seated position at a desk or table. Place your feet flat on the floor, resting your elbow on the desk. Hold the pendulum by the end of the chain between your thumb and index finger. Simply allow it to hang for a moment or two. Now circle

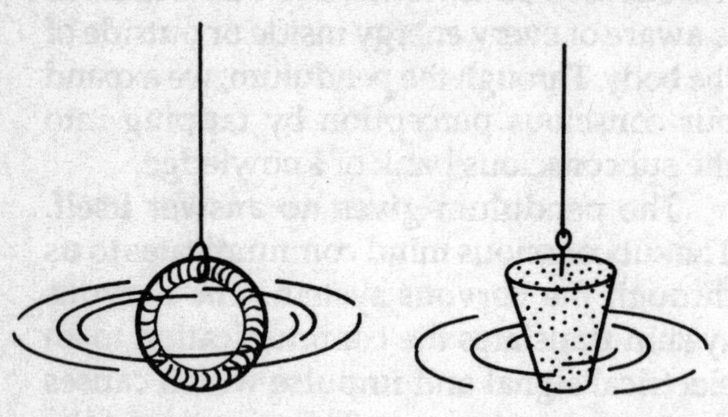

Simple ring on a string   A cork, needle and thread

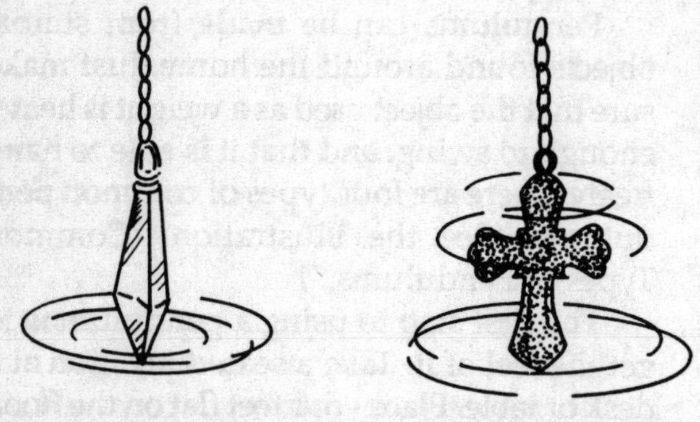

Quartz crystal pendulum   Common necklace cross & chain

Common Types of Pendulums

it gently in a clockwise direction. Allow it to stop and then rotate it in a counterclockwise direction. Next, move it vertically, horizontally and diagonally. Become comfortable with its feel.

The next step is to teach it how to respond to the subconscious mind. It is like programming your computer. You are telling it what kind of feedback you expect, so that you will be able to understand its movement when you ask it questions. Draw similar figures on a piece of paper and lay it on the desk, dangling the pendulum over its middle. (See the illustration "Programming the Pendulum Movements.")

Tell yourself out loud, "When I ask a question and the answer is yes, my subconscious will make the pendulum move (direction)." You could follow the method we've illustrated here, in which case "YES" corresponds to the vertical axis. At this point, swing your pendulum gently in the vertical line. You are simply programming the subconscious mind how to move the pendulum in response to your questions. If you wish, you can use the circular movements as depicted in the bottom diagram. Do this several minutes a day for at least a week.

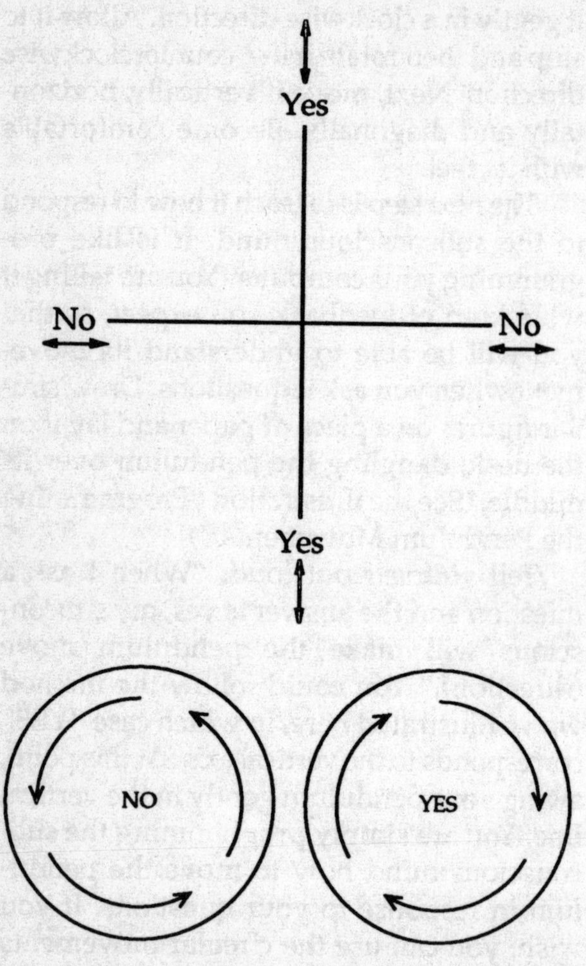

Programming Pendulum Movements

As you begin to program your pendulum, test it. Prove to yourself that it works. Rest your elbow comfortably and let the pendulum hang still. Think to yourself the word, "YES." Repeat it in your mind and let your eyes look up and down the "YES" line. Do this until the pendulum swings up and down on its own. Stay relaxed. Now think to yourself, "STOP." As the pendulum comes to a rest, repeat the procedure using the "NO" line.

Once you become comfortable with the pendulum and its operation, you can use it to ask your subconscious and your intuitive self what color(s) may be needed. Construct a small chart that has a list of colors (see the illustration "Determining Colors with a Pendulum"). Hanging the pendulum over each color, ask the question, "Does __________ need this color?" (Put in your name or the name of someone with which you are doing a healing.) If the pendulum answers, "YES," pay attention to how strong its movement is. The intensity and speed indicate how much of that particular color is needed. The faster the movement, the more of that color you "need."

Go through each of the colors on the chart with your pendulum. Make sure you phrase your question so that it can be answered "YES" or "NO." Then proceed to apply the color treatment through any of the ways discussed in this book.

After the treatment, you may wish to check and see if more treatment is necessary. Ask your pendulum such questions as, "Does _______ need more red?", "Is five minutes enough of a treatment?", etc. With practice, you will learn to use the pendulum to test and verify the effects of your color treatments with great accuracy.

Determining Color Therapy Through Kinesiology

Kinesiology is the study of muscle movements in the body—voluntary and involuntary—and their interactions with the rest of our energy system. Part of the study of kinesiology involves the connection between muscles and the electrical system of the body. As the muscles move, contracting and extending, electrical energy is released. If muscles are overworked, too much electrical energy is released, and soreness, weakness, and tiredness can result. If muscles are not worked enough, too much magnetic energy accumulates, resulting in softer muscle tissue and the accumulation of fat around the muscles.

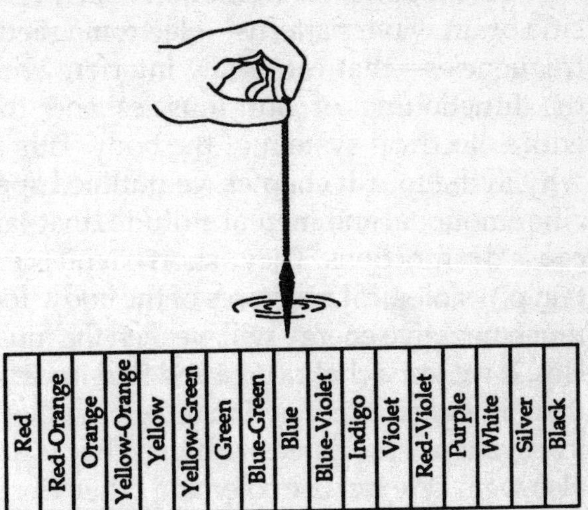

Determining Colors with a Pendulum

Once you are comfortable with the pendulum, use a color chart to help you determine the color(s) most beneficial for therapy and health. Allow the pendulum to hang freely over each color in turn, asking the question, "Is this color needed?" The pendulum movement will let you know the answer. After the treatment, you can go back and check the colors once more, simply by using the "YES" and "NO" questioning approach. "Is more red needed?" "Does _____ need more violet?" The pendulum is helping you to access your intuitive mind so that the color can be applied more beneficially.

Our thoughts and emotions elicit specific brain wave patterns—electromagnetic frequencies—that can easily interfere with the functioning of our muscles and the entire electrical system of the body. This is why in the fourth chapter we outlined specific emotional and mental attitudes that can cause dysfunctions. They "short circuit" certain physiological processes of the body. Too much negative energy will weaken the muscles. If we test a chakra area and find it weak, there is a great likelihood that the physiological systems associated with that chakra are also weak. We can use color and other vibrational remedies to balance it and strengthen it.

Muscle-testing gives us tangible feedback about our energies and their health. It is not foolproof, but it provides a starting point for greater self-awareness and responsibility.

Muscle-testing is simple. You do not need extensive knowledge about the body's muscular system to do it. You will need to know the general location of the chakra centers of the body. Here's how to muscle-test:

1. Choose a chakra center to be tested. If you wish, you can test them all, but for now it is important to experience how the process works.

2. Have the individual to be tested to extend his/her arm out to the side. His/her other hand should be placed over the chakra point to be tested. Refer to the illustration "Determining Color Through Muscle-Testing."

3. Place your own hand upon the wrist of the other person's outstretched arm. As you apply pressure downward, have the other person resist you. Do not force their arm down with your strength. Rather, apply pressure for only a couple inches, applying the pressure gradually and releasing it gradually. The muscle response will either be strong in the first part, locking into place, or it will give. Does the arm lock or does it feel mushy? With practice you will be able to attune to the strength and resistance.

4. Having determined the present strength of the chakra, it is time to demonstrate how it can be short-circuited by our thoughts and emotions. This is an essential step in helping people overcome doubts they may have about the effectiveness of various holistic health practices. Using the guides from chapter four, have the individual focus upon one of the emotional or mental attitudes that can create dysfunction within a chakra center.

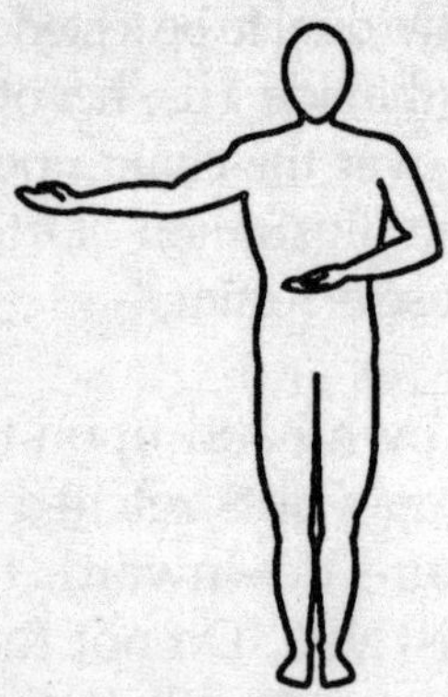

Determining Color Through Muscle-Testing

Begin by having the individual extend one arm and place the hand of the other over a chakra point to be tested. This establishes a connection between the chakra and the muscle strength. With steady pressure upon the wrist of the extended arm, push down. The resistance provides tangible feedback.

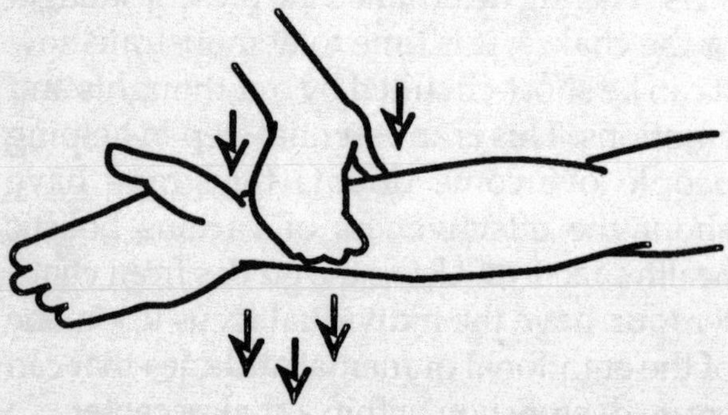

5. When the emotion or mental attitude is in mind, retest the individual, as you did in steps one through three. You will find that the individual's muscle response will be noticeably weaker. This demonstrates tangibly that emotions and attitudes affect us on physiological levels. This is also why it is important to be aware of the range of emotions you are exposed to and experience throughout the day. If you don't re-balance those chakras affected by the emotions, physical dis-ease is more likely to manifest.

6. Having demonstrated how the chakras and the corresponding physical responses can be short-circuited, it is important to demonstrate how vibration, in the form of color, can help. This is a good process to go through before applying any color therapy. It eliminates doubts and it makes the individual more receptive to the treatment.

7. Using any of the color healing methods in this book, apply color to the tested chakra for 15 to 30 seconds. Now employ the muscle-testing once more. If you have correctly used the color healing method there will be a noticeable improvement.

This muscle-testing can also be done on yourself. It can be used with any muscle of the body. The electrical system of the body and the chakras are tied intimately to the functions of all muscles in the body, voluntary and involuntary. The self-testing method should be done daily, as it does not take much time and it prevents imbalances from building up.

One of the easiest ways to self-test is to use your fingers. Mentally bring your mind to focus upon a particular chakra point of the body. You do not have to place your hands on it for yourself. Concentrate upon it. As you concentrate upon this chakra center, bring the index finger and thumb of one hand together tightly. (See the illustration, "Muscle-testing Yourself.") With the index finger of your other hand, try and separate the circled thumb and finger. If the chakra is weak, the thumb and index finger will be easily separated. If it is strong, they will stay together.

For self-testing, it is beneficial to balance your entire chakra system first. Then muscle-test, using your fingers. Learn to recognize when the energies are strong. Muscle-test periodically throughout the day. Is the resistance as strong as when you are bal-

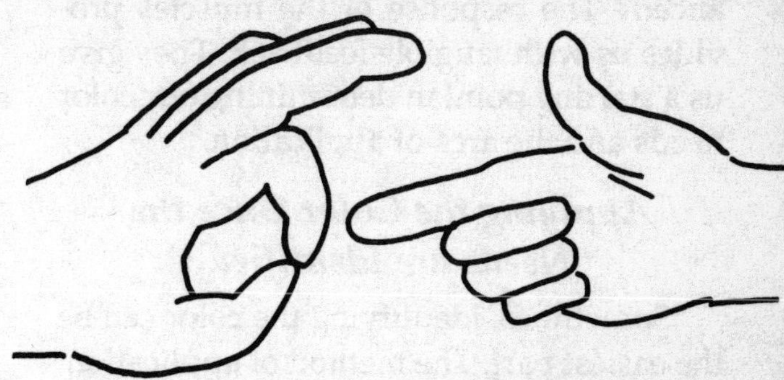

If the chakra you focus upon is strong and balanced, the response of whatever muscle you test will also be strong and balanced. It should be difficult to separate the thumb and index finger when testing a balanced chakra.

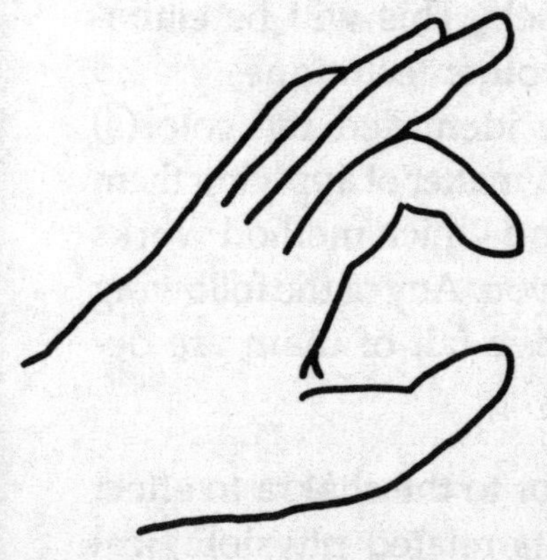

If the chakra being focused upon is weak, then the thumb and index finger are easily separated Applying a beneficial color to that chakra will strengthen both the chakra and the muscle response.

Muscle-Testing Yourself

anced? The response of the muscles provides us with tangible feedback. They give us a starting point in determining our color needs and the area of application.

Applying the Color Once the Needs are Identified

Sometimes, identifying the color can be the easiest part. The method of application, the length of application, and other factors can be confusing. Throughout this book you are given a variety of color application techniques. In chapter two we discussed one which involves using your own hands and thoughts to send colored energy to another person or to yourself. This will be elaborated upon, as will other techniques.

Once you have identified the color(s) needed, it is simply a matter of applying them in some fashion. Find which method works most effectively for you. Any of the following methods are effective (all of them are described in this book):

- Applying color to the chakra to effect a change in its related physiological element.

- Projecting a color through your hands into the area of the body that is unbalanced.

- Performing color breathing to fill your body with the appropriate colored energy.

- Drinking color-charged water.

- Laying colored cloth swatches upon the chakra or area of body.

- Using a slide projector for color therapy.

- Using colored candles to assist in the healing session.

6

COLOR THERAPY WITH AIR AND WATER

Two of the most essential elements of life are air and water. We cannot survive very long without either one. Most people do not drink enough water or get enough fresh air. Simply increasing both will boost the overall energy levels. We can also use both air and water in color therapy to assist the body in healing itself of various conditions.

Fresh air and proper breathing are essential to overall health and vitality. Breathing for the most beneficial effects should be done through the nostrils. Many people have the bad habit of mouth breathing, not realizing that nostril breathing is more natural and healthy. Mouth breathing makes an individual more susceptible to illness. It impairs the overall energy and it can weaken the constitution. Between the mouth and the lungs there is nothing to strain the air.

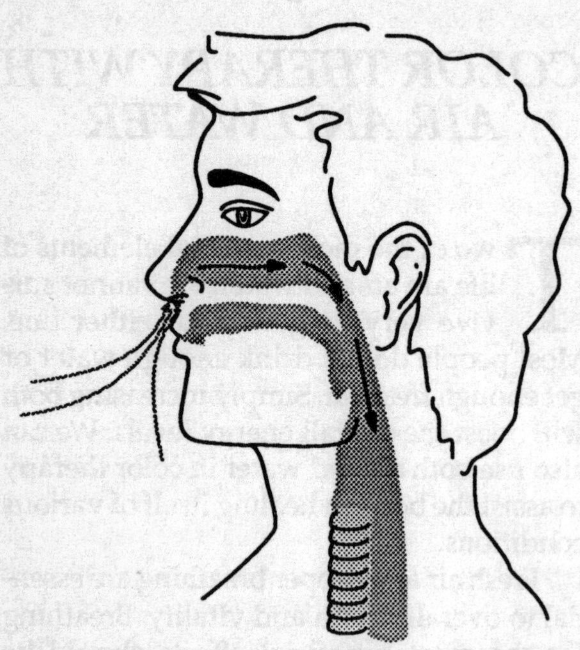

Proper Nostril Breathing

Breathing in through the nostrils is healthier. The nasal passages, with the help of the mucous membranes, filter the air and warm it. An ideal energizing breath involves an inhalation through the nose, with the tongue pressed against the roof of the mouth just behind the upper front teeth. The exhalation is then through the mouth. This activates two major energy pathways, creating an invigorating energy orbit through the body.

Dust, dirt and other impure substances have a clear track to the lungs. Mouth breathing also admits cold air to the lungs which can lead to inflammation of the respiratory organs.

Nostril breathing on the other hand is healthier and more vitalizing to our entire energy system. The nostrils and the nasal passages have small hairs that are designed to filter and sieve the air. The nasal passages also warm the air through the mucous membranes. This makes the air more fit for the delicate organs of the lungs. Breath is then more energizing.

Focused deep breathing helps transform the air we breathe into energy. The vibrancy of that energy is affected by thought and by method. With proper focus, air can be breathed into different parts of the body and transformed into different frequencies of energy.

One of the most beneficial breathing exercises is to use the early morning air to infuse the body with energy. Take a seated position outdoors. Place the tip of the tongue to the roof of the mouth, just behind the upper front teeth. Inhale slowly through the nose for a slow count of five. Hold the breath for a count of five and then exhale slowly for a count of five through the mouth.

Have your eyes closed softly as you perform this exercise. Imagine and visualize this air filling your entire body with invigorating energy that heals and strengthens. Remember that you are also breathing in light and all of the colors it contains. Perform this exercise for 10 to 15 minutes every morning. You will be amazed at how much more vibrant and energized you remain throughout the day. You will become less fatigued and less aggravated by outside energies and intrusions. Performing this rhythmic breathing periodically throughout the day will also balance your system, relieve stress, and restore your overall vitality.

Proper breathing should also involve the diaphragm. Place your hands gently upon your navel. Inhale deeply. Do your hands move outward? Exhale slowly. Do your hands move back in? If so, you are breathing properly from the diaphragm. Many people only breathe from the upper chest, and the hand movements are reversed. In these cases, the air is not taken deeply into the body and less energy and vitality is achieved from breathing.

Another generally beneficial breathing technique is to create an orbit of energy up the back of the body and down the front. In Taoist forms of healing it is often referred to

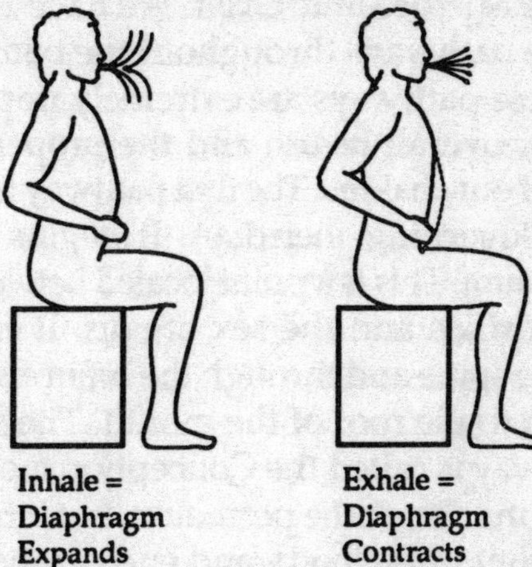

Inhale through the nose for a specified count. Hold the breath for the same count, and then exhale out the mouth for the count.

You should be able to feel the diaphragm expand with each breath.

Proper Rhythmic Breathing

as the Microcosmic Orbit. We have various nerve pathways throughout the body. Two of these pathways are extremely important to our overall health and the proper function of our chakras. The first pathway is called the Governing meridian. It begins at the perineum. This is a point located between the anal orifice and the sex organs. It extends up the spine and through the brain and back down to the roof of the mouth. The second pathway is called the Conception meridian. It begins also at the perineum, but it runs up the front of the body and ends at the tip of the tongue.

The tongue is a trigger. When the tongue is placed against the roof of the mouth behind the front teeth, it connects the two channels of energy. The air that we breath is converted into energy which can then be circulated up the spine and down the front of the body. This circulation is accomplished by focused thought and by proper positioning of the tongue while breathing.

This orbit of energy circles up the spine and back down the front. It energizes the major organs of the body and the entire nervous system, vitalizing and healing them. By working with breath, color and the microcosmic orbit, we can more easily pump energy

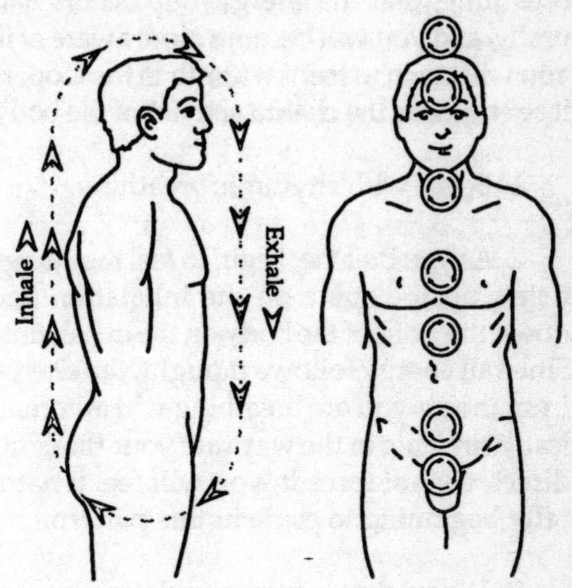

Breathing and the Microcosmic Orbit

Each circle of energy strengthens the chakra, causing stronger clockwise rotation and strengthening related physical energies. To create the microcosmic orbit, perform rhythmic breathing to increase your energy. As you continue to do that, feel the energy circulating up the spine and down the front. As it circulates, feel it energizing your chakra centers. You may even wish to see each orbit change to a different color, one color for each chakra.

into different areas of the body. You will find, as you sit in meditation performing deep breathing, that the energy loop occurs naturally, and you will become more aware of it. You will begin to feel a warmth in the loop, as it strengthens the chakra activity of the body.

1. Begin with rhythmic breathing.

2. As you breathe, begin to feel the energy rising up the spine on the inhalation and down the front of the body on the exhalation. Since all energy follows thought, the energy from the air you are breathing will automatically circulate in the way that your thoughts direct. Do not force it; you will feel it naturally beginning to circle in this pattern.

3. When the energy circulating in this orbit reaches the bottom-most point, visualize this orbit of energy turning and flowing through the body in the color red. Allow the red energy to circle several times and then allow it all to gather in the base chakra, strengthening it. Visualize this center as a powerful vortex of energy that spins energy in and out of the body in a clockwise direction. See it as a miniature dynamo.

4. Focus on the circuit of pure energy again. Now see it as a circuit of orange energy that circulates through the body along this orbital path. After several strong orbits, allow it all to gather in the spleen chakra. Continue this same process with all of the chakras and their colors.

5. After circulating the colors for each chakra, return to focusing and circulating pure energy along this orbit. This exercise is extremely healing and energizing. It helps to prepare the individual to control and direct energy inside the body for various uses. It revitalizes body, mind and spirit. It connects us with our most primal creative energy, helping us to release it more dynamically. It ultimately can be used to control the sexual energy for alchemical purposes.

General Color Breathing

There are simpler ways to do color breathing. Performing color breathing outdoors, or by an open window can be very effective. Remember that air is turned into energy within the body. The frequency and strength of that energy is largely determined by our thoughts. Breathing different colors will assist with different health factors. The key is to determine which colors are needed. Guidelines for determining these colors have already been explored. Refer to previous chapters for specific guidance.

Make yourself comfortable. A seated position may be more comfortable. Your spine should be erect. Place the tip of the tongue against the roof of the mouth just behind the front teeth. Inhale slowly through the nostrils for a count of five or six. Hold that breath for a slow count of 12. Then exhale slowly through the mouth for a slow count of five or six. Establish a slow rhythm.

Now, as you breathe in, see and feel the air coming in as a particular color. See and feel it filling your whole body. See and feel it balancing and healing whatever condition you are wanting to correct. If unsure as to the color, breathe in pure, crystalline white light. You may also simply breath the seven colors of the rainbow to balance your overall system.

Breathing the color for three to five minutes can have a wonderful effect. Different colors, even when being breathed, will elicit different effects:

Red Breath—

Energizing and warming; helps with colds and sinuses; drying to mucous membranes.

Pink Breath—

Beneficial to skin conditions; puffiness; eases loneliness.

Orange Breath—

Balances emotions; can ease respiratory conditions; awakens creativity; restores joy of life; orange and pink combinations (peachy colors) are good for muscles.

Yellow Breath—

Assists you in learning more easily; eases indigestion and gas; the gold shade of yellow is an overall healing color and is beneficial for inner head problems.

Green Breath—

Eases nervous conditions; awakens greater sense of prosperity; pale green is good for improved vision; helps in overcoming bad habits.

Blue Breath—

Calming; awakens artistic talents; eases respiratory problems; generally healing for all children.

Dark Blue Breath—

Accelerates healing and mending after surgery; helps heal bones when combined with tinge of green (teal blue); helps to open intuition.

Turquoise Breath—

Helpful for respiratory conditions; arthritis; can be combined with pink to assist in overcoming bad eating habits.

Violet Breath—

Beneficial to skeletal problems; purifying; helps detoxify the body; awakens spiritual attunement.

Purple Breath—

Helpful in detoxifying the system; helps overcome strong obsessions and negative feelings; most effective when combined with white.

The techniques to control the breath and activate color energies can easily be adapted for use in healing sessions conducted for another person. We can transmit color healing by breathing upon the individual.

After determining the color most appropriate for the condition, have the individual recline. Locate the troubled area. Gently lay a cloth swatch in the appropriate color over it. As you gently hold it within place, begin rhythmic breathing to increase your energy flow. See and feel yourself filling with that particular color vibration. Lean forward, bringing your mouth close to the cloth swatch. As you exhale, breath heavily upon it. See and feel your colored breath energy penetrating the body and restoring balance. The warmth of the breath serves as a catalyst to activate the color vibrations. Continue this breathing for several minutes or until you intuitively are aware that the healing process has begun.

This color breathing method of healing is very effective in easing and alleviating pain. It is quite effective for headaches, cramps and nerve pains. The same kind of healing can also be effected by breathing color into the chakra area as well.

Color Therapy with Water

Water is almost as essential to us as air. Most people do not drink enough water. One of the most beneficial habits an individual can develop is to drink lots of water everyday. Drinking several tumblers upon arising in the morning and before going to bed is a good practice. It helps to flush out the system.

One of the most common complaints about drinking water comes from those who have trouble with water retention. Unfortunately, these individuals do not understand what their body is doing. When our body does not get enough water, it begins to retain it, shifting into a kind of starvation mode. When we drink lots of water during the day, the body does not feel as if it must retain it; it is no longer "starved" for water.

We can magnetize or charge our water with various color frequencies to assist us in healing and activating various energies within the body. There are several ways of charging water. The first way is to simply take a glass and fill it with water. Hold it in one hand and hold your second hand over the glass about three to five inches from it. Begin rhythmic breathing, and focus upon a particular color. See and feel this color radiating out of your hand and into the water. Concentrate upon instilling the glass of water with the particular healing color vibration. Three to five minutes of concentration will magnetize the water strongly. You can then sip it or take it in various doses to help alleviate a condition.

A second method of charging water uses colored jars. Fill the colored jars with water

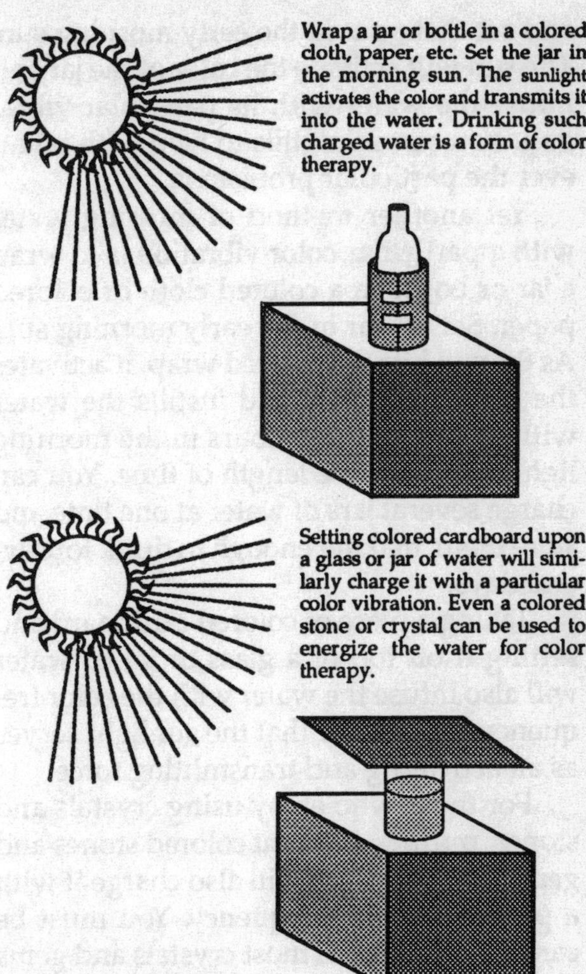

Wrap a jar or bottle in a colored cloth, paper, etc. Set the jar in the morning sun. The sunlight activates the color and transmits it into the water. Drinking such charged water is a form of color therapy.
Setting colored cardboard upon a glass or jar of water will similarly charge it with a particular color vibration. Even a colored stone or crystal can be used to energize the water for color therapy.

Healing with Colored Water

and set them out in the early morning sun. The sun will activate the color of the jar and infuse the water with its particular vibration. You can drink this to help with whatever the particular problem is.

Yet another method of infusing water with a particular color vibration is to wrap a jar or bottle in a colored cloth or colored paper. Set the jar in the early morning sun. As the sun hits the colored wrap, it activates the color frequency and instills the water with it. One to three hours in the morning light is an effective length of time. You can charge several jars of water at one time and store them, making enough to drink for several days.

Taking a piece of colored cardboard and setting it on top of a glass or jar of water will also infuse the water with the color frequency. Remember that the sunlight serves as an activating and transmitting force.

For those who enjoy using crystals and stones, putting different colored stones and gems into the water will also charge it with a particular color frequency. You must be careful with this, as most crystals and gems have a unique electromagnetic frequency, as well as a color energy. This can change how the water affects you, possibly increasing the "charge." A study of various crystals and stones will help you to discern what other kinds of effects the stones could have upon the water, other than its color frequency.

7

PROJECTING COLORS

There are a variety of ways to project colors for therapeutic purposes. Most of these are easily learned and developed by the average individual. We can all learn to apply color therapy to assist in maintaining and restoring our own health and vibrancy. Color therapy is not a substitute for other forms of medicine and therapy, but it is something that enables you to become more active and responsible in your own healing process.

We have already learned that we are more than just physical substance. We are comprised of other, more subtle energy fields. We have also seen that there are ways of interacting with these subtle energies to create changes in physical conditions. For those who are interested in pursuing holistic healing, in incorporating color therapy into their own practices, or for those who see it as a means of helping themselves on physical and subtle levels, the methods in this chapter will be of great benefit.

The Touch of Color

Earlier, we demonstrated how we can radiate energy outward from our hands by breathing and by concentrating our thoughts. This first form of healing with color has always been considered more of a spiritual form. Unfortunately, when you mention that you do spiritual healing, many individuals assume that it is healing based solely upon faith and the healer's alignment with some divine force.

Although the healing touch can be enhanced by faith, its effectiveness is not dependent upon faith or the divine. (Unless one recognizes that the divine operates in each one of us and thus can be accessed by each of us.) How the healing process actually takes place is still poorly understood. Even so, it is important to acknowledge that when we perform certain acts, there will be certain effects. We all have this capability of creating changes within our physical and subtle energies—even if we don't understand it all. It is innate. What we must do is learn the techniques that enables us to awaken and channel it for our various purposes.

Keep in mind that healing always comes from within. It is the patient who heals himself or herself. You may be a catalyst, and an assistant to boost the individual's own recuperative system, but the healing must come from within.

Before you begin to work to heal another person, know what you are going to do. Understand the process. Understand which colors you need to use for the condition. Try and understand the metaphysical causes of the physical dis-ease, and discuss this with the individual. Make no claims. Explain how our energy system operates. Perform some muscle testing to prove it, if necessary, and simply present yourself as someone who would like to help.

Never work on another person if you are tired or ill. Although it's true that when we work to heal another we in turn are healed, working on another while we demonstrate illness can set up mental blocks and hinder the receptivity of the healing colors and energy.

Healing Through Touch

You are becoming a channel of color energy. As you breathe, you pull energy down through you and radiate it out your hands to heal and balance the individual. The energy takes on the frequency of your thoughts and focus. As you concentrate on a particular color, the radiations take that frequency, and the color is absorbed by the person being treated. The process heals and balances, and it awakens your higher intuition and sensitivities. Here are the steps for this technique:

1. Center yourself before you ever begin. Relax. Perform some rhythmic breathing.

2. Have the individual recline in front of you. Extend your hands over the individual about three to six inches.

3. Visualize pure crystalline energy pouring down through the top of your head, filling your body to overflowing. See and feel it pouring down your arms and out your hands.

4. Begin with crystalline white energy. Holding your hands over the crown of the individual's head, see and feel this white light pouring through you and into the other person. See their whole body and energy field becoming charged, strengthened and balanced. Continue this for several minutes. Stop when you feel comfortable with it. Work-

ing with healing helps you to attune to your higher self. Listen to it.

5. Now move to the particular problem area. Continue your rhythmic breathing. Focus your mind on the color needed for the problem. See the energy pouring out through you to that area, balancing and healing it. See it becoming stronger as the color radiations are absorbed. Visualize the energy cleansing, balancing and healing the immediate imbalanced area, as well as the entire system with which it is associated.

6. Next move to the chakra(s) closest to the problem area. For example, if there is stomach upset, begin by working on that particular area of the stomach. Next see the entire digestive system being balanced and healed. Then move your hands and attention to the solar plexus chakra which mediates the energies of the digestive system and the stomach. Project balancing energy to the chakra in its appropriate color.

7. Now move to the base chakra area. Concentrate on radiating red energy to energize and strengthen it. Do this for several minutes. Then move up to each of the seven

chakras, projecting the appropriate colors. This balances the entire chakra system, and it strengthens the overall healing process.

8. To conclude the healing, you may return to the head area and project crystalline white energy through you into the individual. See and feel it pouring into your head and out of your hands, filling the individual's entire being with strength and vibrancy.

Light Projections in Healing

There are a number of ways in which we can use colored lights for therapeutic purposes. The simplest is by using colored light bulbs and sitting under them. As you sit under the lights breathe deeply and regularly, knowing your body will absorb the energy. The variety of colors available in light bulbs is somewhat limited, but there is another way of projecting colored light. We can make our own slides, and using a normal slide projector, project lights in various combinations more simply and quickly. Slide projectors are rather inexpensive, and many can be found in discount stores and pawn shops for next to nothing. The next step is to make your own slides.

Most camera stores have inexpensive

blank slide frames for sale. Colored filter paper of various colors can be cut to fit inside the frame. The colored filter paper can be purchased at a theatrical supply store. It is the most effective. If you do not have access to a theatrical store, many school and office supply stores carry plastic sheets for overhead projectors. These also come in a variety of colors. If nothing else, the clear plastic sheets can be colored with overhead projector pens.

Making the slides is a simple task. Take your empty slide frame and open it up. Now take your filter paper, and cut a square so that it will cover the opening of the slide when the slide frame is closed. There should be enough space left around the color filter so that the two sides of the frame can be glued together. Place drops of glue around the edges of one side of the open frame. Hold the filter in place and close the slide frame over it. Press the two sides together until the glue sticks.

If you wish, you can make several sets of colored slides: The basic set should be for energizing and strengthening of the chakras. It should have the seven colors of the rainbow with it—red, orange, yellow, green, blue, indigo, and violet.

You can also make a set of slides for gen-

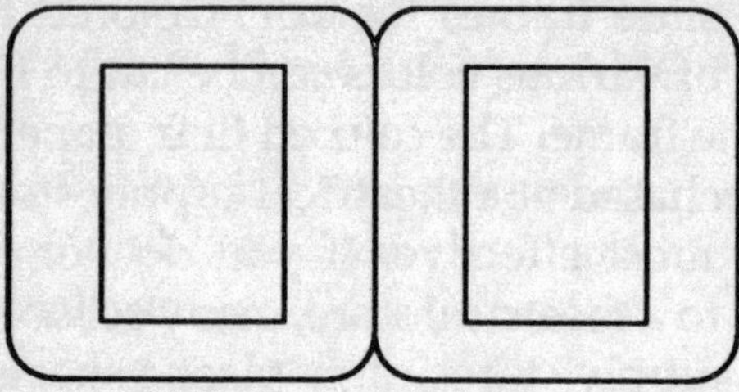

Open the slide frame and cut the filter paper so that it covers the opening in the frame. Leave enough frame space around the filter so that the two sides of the frame can be glued together.

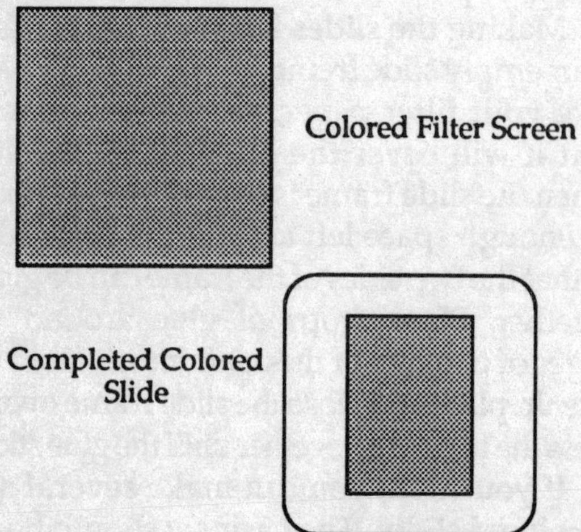

Set the filter over the opening, place glue around the outside edges of the frame and then press together.

Making Your Colored Slides

eral healing purposes. This set includes the basic seven colors, but adds the in-between shades and other colors that may be needed. This set can help fine-tune the chakras and aid in healing more specific conditions. Here are some of the colors this set can include:

Red	Red-orange	Orange
Yellow-orange	Yellow	Yellow-green
Green	Blue-green	Blue
Indigo	Blue-violet	Violet
Red-violet	Lemon	Turquoise
Purple	Magenta	Scarlet

You probably won't find all of these colors available in filter paper. You can still create them by combining different filter papers and including them in the same slide. The light of the projector will blend and activate the colors. The filter paper is thin, so several colors can be combined within the slide frame effectively. These formulas will help you:

Red, yellow and blue are the primary colors. (You should be able to find these in filter paper.) You can combine the primary colors to create the other colors.

Creating Colors Through Combinations

Scarlet:	2 reds
Red-orange:	2 red filters and 1 yellow filter
Orange:	1 red filter and 1 yellow filter
Yellow-orange:	2 yellow filters and 1 red filter
Yellow-green:	2 yellow filters and 1 blue filter
Green:	1 yellow filter and 1 blue filter
Blue-green:	3 blue filters and 1 yellow filter
Turquoise:	2 blue filters and 1 yellow filter
Indigo:	2 blue filters and 1 red filter
Violet:	1 red filter and 1 blue filter
Blue-violet:	2 blue filters and 1 red filter
Red-violet:	2 red filters and 1 blue filter
Magenta:	3 red filters and 1 blue
Purple:	1 yellow filter, 1 red filter and 1 blue filter

Conducting a Color Slide Healing Session

To conduct a color-slide healing session, put the slides into the projector in the order necessary to create the colors you want to use in the healing. Set the projector opposite the person. Have the individual take a seated position. Explain color breathing to the individual and ask him/her to do color breathing as each colored slide is projected upon them. Have them picture the projected light filling, energizing, and healing the particular condition. For a rainbow effect, have the person visualize the colors entering through the crown chakra and filling the entire body.

Go through the necessary colors, leaving each color on the individual for two to three minutes. For chronic conditions, you may wish to do longer treatments. Again, don't be afraid to trust your own intuition in this process.

The session can be ended beneficially in several ways. Using the green light at the end is effective. It balances the energy system of the individual. However, you do not want to use this in conditions that are cancerous or tumorous, as green helps things

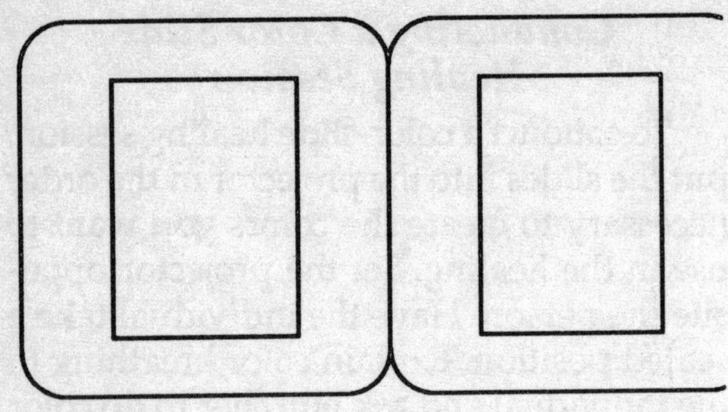

Using Colored Slides to Heal

to grow. You may wish to simply run the color for each chakra, starting with the base and moving to the crown. If you are concerned about the green, substitute a pink or a white light for the heart center.

You can also sit under the lights yourself, if you use a hand control for the projector to control the slides. In this way, you can use the projector to heal and balance yourself. You may even wish to use these slides to assist you in your meditation. Remember, the colors affect more than just the physiological systems of the body. They also activate our subtle energies and levels of consciousness as well. If, for example, you have difficulty relaxing in your meditation, sit under the blue light while meditating. Experiment. Have fun with it. Color projections are powerful and effective.

Long-Distance Color Healing

Absentee or long-distance healing can be an effective tool to assist an individual. Often people are asked to send prayers and healing to others who are not present. This is something that we can enhance through the various color techniques discussed within this book.

The phenomenon of long-distance healing is nothing new. It does transcend logical thought processes, but it in no way transcends reality. Energy operates on all levels and is in many ways not yet understood. That which is referred to as psychic energy is the creative life force of all substance. It surrounds us, penetrates us, and is a part of us. It can be controlled and directed, molded and shaped, stored and used. It can be controlled by the mind.

We know that the human body is a bio-chemical, electromagnetic energy system, but our psychic energy is the basic building block of these. The bio-chemical and the electromagnetic aspects are the physical expressions of our psychic life force. This psychic life force operates on a level that transcends physical time and space.

Quantum physics has done much to explain the phenomenon of psychic energy. It teaches us that all life and all energy expressions are connected. Because we are energy, operating on many levels and in many forms, we cannot move without influencing everything in our universe. Every time we observe something, we are changed, and so is what we are observing. With higher expressions and focuses of energy, time and space are transcended. Thus, in long-distance healing we experience the individual as if he/she were in immediate proximity, regardless of actual time and location.

Colors can be used to assist us in concentrating, tuning, and transmitting healing energies. They also assist us in achieving a transcendent level of consciousness so that we can employ a more concentrated focus of our psychic energy. We are developing a controlled use of mind through the power of color.

For long-distance healing, it is beneficial to have a "witness." A witness is a term that has come to be used in the field of radionics. It is "anything which will psychically represent the subject."* A witness can be a photo,‡ a signature, a blood specimen, hair clippings, nail clippings or anything which can provide a link between you and the person to whom you wish to direct the colors. The witness helps us to link the rational and the intuitive levels of the mind, thus serving to awaken the process of sending energy at a distance.

The witness assists us in creating a thought form and in directing it toward the individual more effectively. Through the witness, you are more easily able to establish resonance. It serves to awaken the connection beyond physical levels. It brings the individual "to mind." The healing energy can then be sent regardless of time and space.

Take time before sending the healing energy to determine which color(s) will be most beneficial. If unsure, send crystalline white light. You may wish to use your pendulum to determine the colors needed. Hold your left hand over the picture (or witness)

---

* Charles W. Cosimano, *Psionics 101*. (St. Paul: Llewellyn Publications, 1986), p. 82.

‡ A polaroid photograph is considered most effective by many people, in that it will capture the entire positive and negative ion field around the individual, while a photo developed from a negative will only capture half of the field. Thus, it is not considered as strong of a link.

and with the right hand using the pendulum, ask questions concerning the colors needed by the individual.

Once the healing colors are discerned, we must then proceed to project the healing energies. There are several effective ways of doing this.

1. You may simply do it through your ability to visualize. Hold the witness between your two hands. If you do not have a witness, hold the individual's image within your mind. Begin rhythmic breathing. As you focus on the individual, see and feel the energy radiating through you and out to him/her. Visualize this color surrounding them and permeating their system. Visualize the condition being balanced and healed. Perform this for about ten minutes.

2. You may wish to use the slide projector. Tape the picture (or witness) to a white piece of poster board. Shine the colors of the seven chakras upon it for about thirty seconds each. Then focus the primary healing color upon the picture, and leave it on for ten to fifteen minutes.

You can confidently go about your business, knowing the color radiations will seek out the individual. This is very effective to do at night, when you know the individual is likely to be asleep. There are less distractions, and the effects of the colors are more easily absorbed.

3. You may also wish to use the color radiations from candles to assist you in projecting long-distance healing energies. (Use the following chapter as a guideline.) Simply place the witness next to a particular candle or in one of the candle healing patterns described in the next chapter. Do this for 15 to 30 minutes per day.

When conducting any healing, it is always good to affirm that the healing manifest "for the good of all, according to the free will of all." In this manner, the healing occurs in the most beneficial way for the individual's growth. We do not have the right to intrude upon the free will of others. Since this technique is a dynamic way of affecting people in subtle, often unnoticed, yet very real ways, we must be cautious.

Opinions differ as to whether or not one should project healing toward another without their permission. I am of the school of taking great personal responsibility for one's life and actions, and the only one who knows what is ultimately best for that individual is that individual. Everyone has the right to make mistakes. It is often through our mistakes that our greatest growth can occur. If we interfere, we may rob the individual of a learning experience critical to his or her evolution. Besides, it takes hardly any energy to ask someone if you can help.

These are not hard and fast rules. Obviously, if there is someone under your care—such as children—you act in accordance with what you as an adult know is best. There are always exceptions, but you must make your decisions, especially your healing ones, with a willingness to take full responsibility for the consequences of your actions—positive or negative. If you cannot do this, then you do not need to be dabbling in the healing energies.

Keep in mind that you are not practicing medicine—there are many laws against diagnosing and prescribing. We cannot prescribe colors like we can medication. When we use the tools of vibrational healing we are employing preventive care, along with holistic maintenance. Taking money for using color on someone must be approached cautiously, as the laws are very strict about practicing medicine without a license. I personally do not charge for my healing sessions, nor do I take donations. I do make a suggestion that the individual either donate to a charity or pass a favor on anonymously to someone else. I do know a number of licensed massage therapists who employ color in their work, but it is used as a tool within the massage process, and as they are licensed, there is no problem.

Do not be afraid to experiment. The extent of the healing effects of color is as yet undetermined. In fact, they may never truly be defined, in that color can be used to enhance any method of healing—traditional or nontraditional.

8

HEALING WITH CANDLES

Fire has always been regarded as something holy. In many ancient cultures, the manner in which smoke melted into the air was magical. The origin of fire was just as magical and mysterious. In most societies, fire first belonged to the gods, and the tales and myths of the great fire-stealers still live today within our books and lore. Prometheus and the creation of humanity is but one example. (Prometheus stole fire from the gods to give it to humanity.)

Fire operates in all of our lives in physical and subtle ways. The fires from the sun sustain life upon the earth. The fires of passion bring inspiration and creativity. Fire operates in all aspects of life. From volcanic fires to the fires of ordinary body heat, from the solar fires to the fires of intellect, fire's presence is felt nearly everywhere.

Candles have been used for metaphysical purposes for about as long as fire has been around. The candle is a very powerful symbol for the activation of more fire and light in our lives—on physical and subtle levels. When we use the fires of candles, we are participating in the ritual of fire that has existed throughout the ages, from the lighting of the stars to the lighting of hearthstones of companionship and community.

The practice of using candles for healing should be seen as an ancient rite of creation. When you light the candle, imagine you are creating light where there was no light before, bringing warmth and healing where it is needed. This imaging in itself is extremely healing. See the unlit candle as the unlit essence of life energy in the physical body that awaits a renewing touch of fire to help restore health to body and soul.

Fundamental Rules for Candle Use

1. The color of the candle and its vibrational force is activated, released and amplified when it is lit. As the candle burns, the color is released into the surrounding area and affects those within that area.

2. The color of the candle that you use is determined by the kind of healing needed. Consult the list that was of colors that correspond to different conditions given earlier in this book.

3. All candles should be cleansed and blessed before their use. This serves to cleanse the candle of any negativity it may have accumulated and absorbed during its making. It strengthens the color so that it works far more effectively for your purpose. This process is called "dressing the candle."

This dressing of the candle is done with an oil. There are several candle-anointing oils on the market. You can also use a simple olive oil. Always rub the candle in the same direction. For healing candles, it is beneficial to rub them from bottom to top. This is symbolic of bringing the color out of the candle and into the atmosphere.

Do not worry if you do not have an oil to use. Simply using a strong affirmation that relates to your purpose or reciting a favorite prayer as you dress the candle is effective. It prepares the candle, and it prepares you.

4. Once you have used a candle for a specific purpose, it should not be used for something else. This will set up conflicting vibrations.

5. Any candle will be effective. For longer, more sustained effects, church candles can be quite effective. They come encased in glass containers and they can burn for a week at a time.

6. Do not use candles to interfere with the free will of another. The rebound effect is never very pleasant.

7. Extinguishing the candle should be the last act in the healing process. It should be performed with strong intention, as if you are firmly setting and locking the healing energy in place. It is preferable that breath not be used to extinguish the candle. Breath, like fire, is creative, and a creative force should not be used to extinguish another creative force. Use a small cup or tin-foil cone to extinguish the flame.

Candle Colors

Candles have tremendous thought forms associated with them. The color of the candles will elicit therapeutic effects in the same manner as colored cloth or colored light. Candles have not only been used for healing but also for prayer, meditation, and magical purposes. It is a good idea to understand these metaphysical associations with candles before you use them.

White—

The white candle is a symbol of purity and power. It amplifies the effects of any other color candle it is burned with. It promotes cleansing and awakens hope. It can be used to initiate new energy movement in healing or in other avenues. Unless it is an extremely cheap candle, when a white candle smokes, it indicates that the negativity in the area is being burnt off. When the smoking ceases, the area is cleansed.

Black—

The black candle is very powerful. It is also one of the most protective. It can be used to bring a person back down to earth. It can also be used in various rituals to uncover secrets and for understanding the purpose of sacrifices we have made. It can be used in meditation to help us find the light within the dark. It is stabilizing and awakens greater responsibility. It is most effective when burnt with a white candle. Too much black can manifest depression.

Red—

The red candle is a symbol of love and health and the attainment of ambitions. It is the color and candle of passion and sexual potency which are expressions of our primal life force.

Pink—

The pink candle is a symbol of love and success. It awakens a consciousness of clean living and honor. It stimulates purity of intention and it can awaken a vision of truth and success.

Orange—

The orange candle is a symbol of joy and creativity. It can be used with meditations to stimulate spiritual attainment. It can help to attract people, animals, and other things you want in your life.

Yellow and Gold—

Yellow is the color of the flame of the candle with which we meditate. In it we can learn to see the fulfillment of our desires.

The gold shades assist in understanding and stimulating dream activity.

Green—

This is the candle of growth and movement. It balances the energies of the body and mind. It can help open levels of consciousness which are aware of the nature spirits in our life. It can stimulate greater youthfulness, abundance and fertility.

Blue—

The blue candle is a symbol of spiritual understanding. It awakens our innate abilities to perceive. It is also a symbol of life, and it awakens within the consciousness a greater faith in life's processes. It is powerfully healing for children. Blue candles have been known to be burned in various rituals to bring in quick money.

Grey and Silver—

This candle color is a symbol of clarity. You can meditate upon it to see how best to initiate new activities. It awakens that level of the subconscious mind that is aware of how the wheels of life are turning for you. It is a good candle to burn when studying astrology as it assists us in understanding our stellar influences. It awakens our most innate primal intuition.

Brown—

Brown is a neutral candle. It is grounding. It can awaken greater discernment and certainty. It can also be meditated upon to help uncover lost articles. It is a color associated with St. Anthony who is the patron saint of lost things.

Violet and Purple—

These are symbols of spirituality, power and mastery. They awaken success, elevation and attainment of spiritual desires.

Healing Methods with Candles

When we light a candle, the color energy is released into the atmosphere. There it can be absorbed by the individual. Simply being in the area of the candle is enough to allow you to be affected. The energy released from the candle will be absorbed through your auric field and taken into the body itself. The more focused you are on that process, the quicker and more effective it is. Breathing in the energy will also amplify the effects.

One of the most beneficial and powerful means of using candles in healing is by arranging them in geometric layouts around the individual. The geometry of energy also has dynamic effects. Its interactions with the electromagnetic fields of humans serves as the basis of mandalas and talismans.

Different geometric shapes will alter and enhance the effects of the colors. It simply involves understanding what the geometric layout will do, and then using that layout to arrange the candles around the individual to be healed. On the following two pages, you can see six basic layouts for candle therapy. They are all very powerful.

The Triangle—

The triangle is an amplifier. It increases the power of the healing force of whatever color candle is being used. It also makes the color more cleansing.

The Square—

Setting candles in the formation of a square around the individual stabilizes the entire physiological system. It calms and settles. It grounds and focuses the basic life force of the color being used.

Healing Layouts with Candles

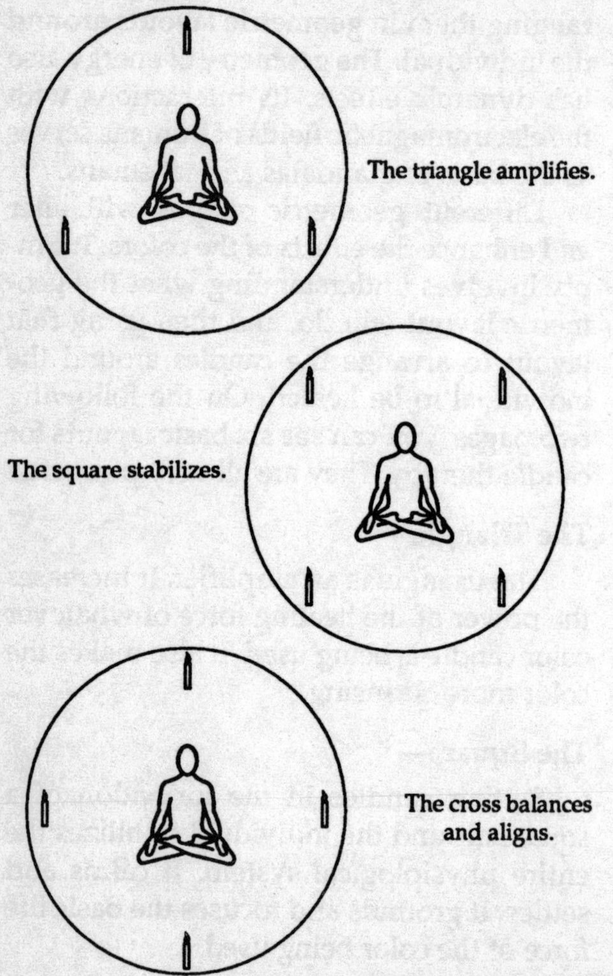
The triangle amplifies.
The square stabilizes.
The cross balances and aligns.

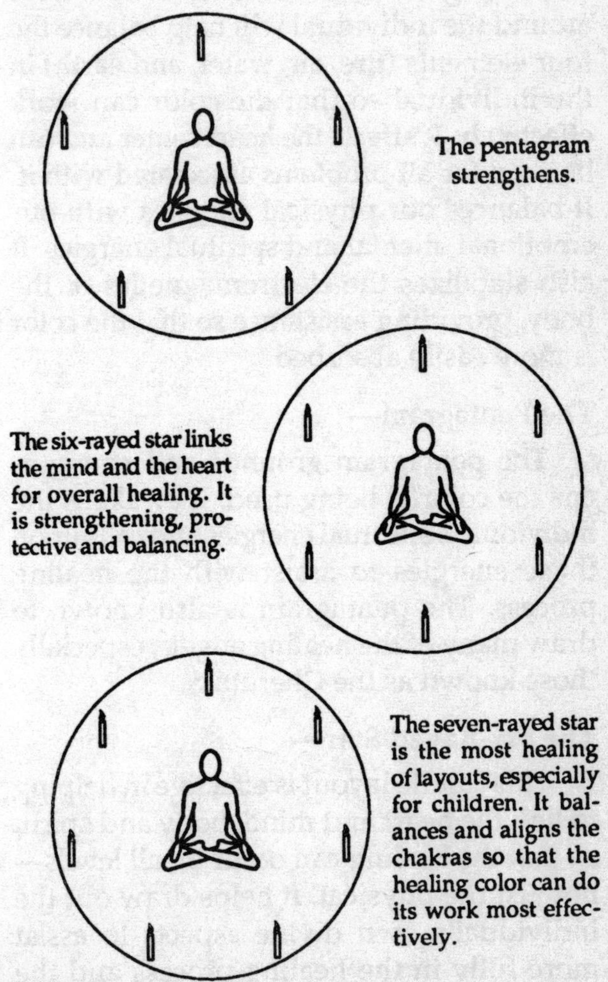

The pentagram strengthens.

The six-rayed star links the mind and the heart for overall healing. It is strengthening, protective and balancing.

The seven-rayed star is the most healing of layouts, especially for children. It balances and aligns the chakras so that the healing color can do its work most effectively.

The Cross—

Placing candles in the form of a cross around the individual will help balance the four elements (fire, air, water, and earth) in the individual so that the color can work effectively. It affects the heart center and can be used for all problems associated with it. It balances our physical energies with our emotional, mental and spiritual energies. It also stabilizes the electromagnetics of the body, providing assistance so that the color is more easily absorbed.

The Pentagram—

The pentagram grounds and strengthens the color(s) being used. It awakens the individual's spiritual energies and calls upon those energies to assist with the healing process. The pentagram is also known to draw many of the healing angels, especially those known as the Cherubim.

The Six-Rayed Star—

This candle layout is effective in helping to link the heart and mind, body and spirit, so that the healing can occur on all levels—not just the physical. It helps draw out the individual's own divine aspects to assist more fully in the healing process and the absorption of the color. It is strengthening and protective.

The Seven-Rayed Star—

This layout is one of the most healing of candle layouts, especially for children. It balances and aligns all of the chakras so that the healing color can work most effectively. It is soothing to emotional and mental attitudes that may have precipitated the physical illness. It amplifies the healing energies of the colors.

The first task in healing with candles, as in any form of color healing, is to determine which color is needed. It may even be several colors. When we use candle layouts, we do not have to use just one color. We can use several colors simultaneously. We can either place a different colored candle in separate positions in the layout or we can set the various colors side by side at each position in the layout. Experiment and find what works best for you.

Having decided on the layout and the color(s), have the individual sit or recline in the middle of the layout. (You can us these same techniques for self-healing as well.) Light the candles with intention. See the lighting of the candles as a creative act that is going to bring light, color and energy to the condition.

As the individual being worked with sits within the layout, begin rhythmic breathing. As you inhale, visualize yourself drawing the color into your body and balancing the condition. Stay relaxed and breathe slowly. Allow the fire-charged color to work smoothly and naturally. Know that your system is being healed and strengthened through this process.

Fifteen to twenty minutes is powerfully effective. You may wish to do this first thing in the morning and the last thing before you go to bed. The effects are cumulative. They stabilize, build, and support your entire energy system. Do this daily until the condition is relieved. Continue a day or two after just to provide extra strength to that area.

Some individuals will continue the treatments daily until the candles have burnt themselves out. Again, experiment. There may be times where you will feel better doing it that way, but there will also be times when it won't be necessary, and undergoing one or two treatments is all that you need. Trust your intuition and your body's response and feedback.

Absent Healing with Candles

We can use candles and layouts to do long distance healings, as well. Again it is good to have a witness (a photo or something the person has touched) to assist in the process. If you do not have a witness, write the individual's name and address on a piece of paper. Then, take a plain white taper candle, dress it, (anointing it with oil to cleanse and bless it), and visualize it as a symbol of the spiritual and physical essence of the one to whom you are going to send healing energies.

Place the white candle on top of the witness (or the paper with the individual's name and address).

Next, arrange the colored candles according to the layout you have chosen, placing the white taper candle in the middle. Light the white candle, visualizing the energies of the individual it represents becoming more vibrant and full of life.

Light the colored candles. See and visualize the person being filled with the healing energies of the candle light. You may leave the candles to burn for ten to fifteen minutes, or you may wish to stay and add your visualizations to the candle projec-

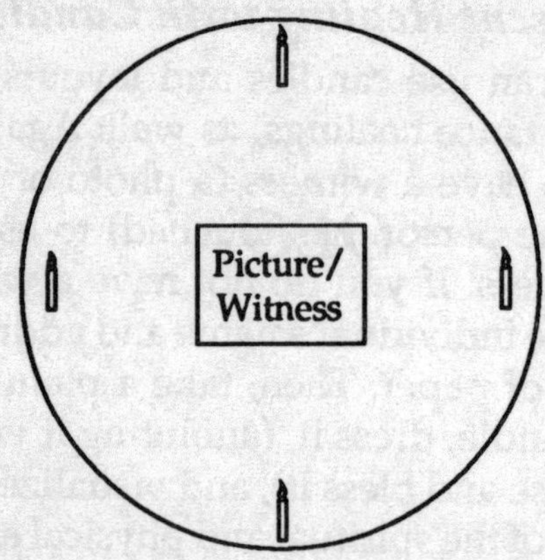

Absent Healing with Candles

Place the witness in the middle of the layout and arrange the colored candles accordingly. The color vibrations are then projected and aligned through the witness to the individual. You may wish to use a white taper candle to represent the witness. Simply light it and set it on top of the witness. This strengthens the process.

---

tions. You may even wish to place yourself in the layout, holding the witness and projecting colors from within the healing layout. Again, experiment. You will find that different methods of healing are necessary for different people. Since we each have our own unique energy system, the healing process must be adjusted accordingly.

9

THE TREE OF COLORS

So far we have discussed some of the more traditional ways to understand and practice color healing. These were from a theosophical perspective, although they have been adapted and adopted into most major systems of metaphysics. However, it is by no means the only system of healing with colors.

No one system is any better or more effective than another. What is important is that you find a system that works for you and with which you are comfortable. The more significance you can personally attach to it, the more receptive you will be to experiencing the healing influence of the color vibrations.

Different traditions had their own color correspondences. For example, astrological traditions assign specific colors to the various planets and signs of the zodiac. (Refer

The Astrological Tradition of Colors: I

Planets	Parts of the Body Ruled	Colors
Sun	Vitality, circulatory system, heart	Oranges, golds
Moon	Breasts, stomach, ovaries, body rhythms	Silvers, greens
Mercury	Nervous system, hands, lungs, respiration	Metallic blues
Venus	Physical appearance (hair, skin, etc.), reproduction	Pastel blues and greens
Mars	Red corpuscles, muscles male genitals	Scarlet and magenta
Jupiter	Liver, hips, thighs, cell nutrition	Deep blue-purples, indigo
Saturn	Skin, bones, teeth, joints, hearing	Black, dark browns and greens
Uranus	Cones and rods in eyes	Electric blues and silvers
Neptune	Pineal gland, chakras	Sea greens, smokey greys
Pluto	Regenerative forces of the reproductive system	Magenta

The Astrological Tradition of Colors: II

Signs of Zodiac	Parts of the Body	Colors
Aries	Head, face brain	Reds
Taurus	Neck, throat, thyroid	Light blues and pastels
Gemini	Hands, shoulders, arms, lungs	Slate blue, lemon yellow
Cancer	Stomach, breasts	Silvers, greens
Leo	Heart, back	Orange, gold
Virgo	Intestines, bowels	Deep blues
Libra	Kidneys, ovaries	Soft pinks and blues
Scorpio	Sex organs, bladder, nose	Deep yellows, bright reds
Sagittarius	Hips, thighs, muscles	Deep blues
Capricorn	Knees, joints, skin	Blacks, browns, dark greens
Aquarius	Calves, ankles, eyes	Electric blues, pale yellows and greens
Pisces	Feet, toes, lymph glands	Sea greens, silvers

(The signs and the planets can indicate a greater propensity for problems in their corresponding body parts, especially if they are found in the sixth house of the astrological chart. The sixth house is the house of health, work and service.)

to the "Astrological Tradition" charts.) Since the signs and planets rule different parts of the body, the astrological colors can be used to assist the healing of those areas. We can still employ the same healing techniques described earlier. We simply adjust the colors to the system with which we are more comfortable.

One of the most effective alternative color-healing systems is that of the mystical Qabala. The Qabala is an ancient form of mysticism with many philosophical and pragmatic dimensions. On one level, it teaches how the universe was formed through ten stages. On a more practical level, it teaches how to access different levels of our consciousness so that we can tap our personal energies and the energies of the universe more effectively.

The Tree of Life is the primary symbol and image for working with the system of the Qabala. It is a diagram with ten levels. Each level represents a specific level of the subconscious mind. Each of these levels is connected to different physiological processes, as well as creative and metaphysical processes. Over time, each of these levels has come to be associated with many different attributes, including specific colors. These correspondences, when utilized, properly activate a level within our subconscious mind. This triggers certain kinds of responses on physical and spiritual levels.

This book does not intend to explore all of these correspondences and their effects. For further information, you may wish to consult the author's earlier books on the Qabala (*Simplified Magic* and *Imagick*). In this chapter, we will concern ourselves only with how to use the Tree of Life in color healing. It is an alternate system, but it is powerfully effective.

A tree is an ancient symbol, and it is easily adapted as a metaphor for the human condition of health. The tree represents things that grow and evolve. It is the bridge between the heavens and the earth. Like the roots and trunk of the tree, humans have their health foundation in the physical body. We must pay attention to our more subtle expressions of energy as well. We cannot just focus on the physical body or the roots of our tree.

Trees must be pruned to bear fruit. They need good soil, clean air, and water. The trunk and the upper branches are just as important to the health of the tree as the roots. A tree is liable to disease from insects, pollutants, and other outside sources. They will eventually work their way down from the upper branches into the root system. All of this affects the tree's ability to bear fruit.

The same is true of humans. If we don't keep our our spiritual, mental, and emotional energies balanced, they will eventually work themselves down into our physical bodies, manifesting dis-ease. We must learn to work with our energies on all levels. This is why in the next chapter we will explore four levels of colors for the Tree of Life healing work. There is a color to help ease every problem —whether it's spiritual, mental, emotional or physical.

Different levels of the subconscious mind control and mediate different energies of the body. The difficulty is in determining which level controls what bodily functions and then determining how to activate that level of the subconscious more consciously. This is where the Qabalistic Tree of Life comes into play.

There are ten levels in the Tree of Life. (See the illustration "The Qabalistic Tree of Life.") In the illustration, the traditional Hebrew title for each level has been given, along with its translation. Each is a symbol of a level within the subconscious mind.

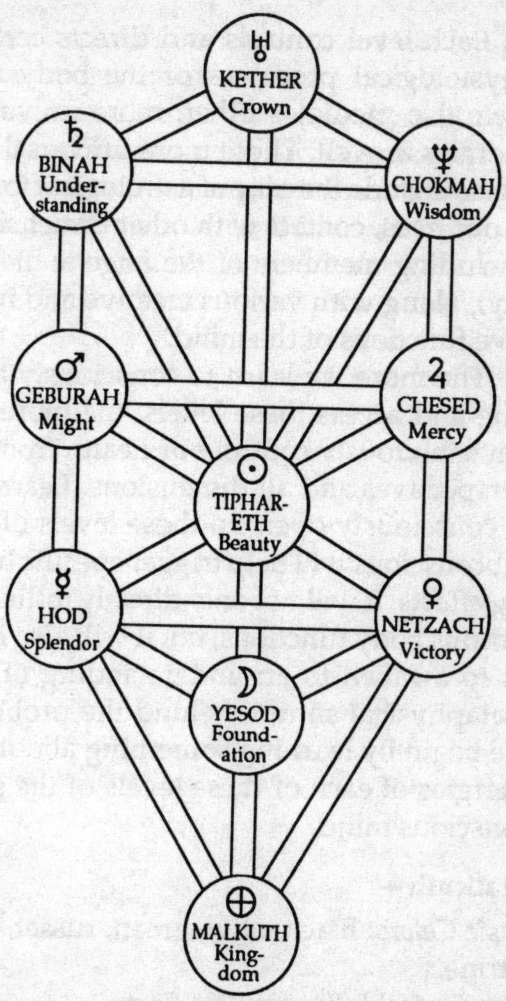

The Qabalistic Tree of Life

Each level controls and directs certain physiological processes of the body and each also mediates other, more universal energies as well. These more universal energies include the play of astrological forces in our lives, contact with other dimensions (including members of the angelic hierarchy), along with various creative and intuitive functions of the mind.

The more we learn to consciously activate and access these levels, the more we can consciously control our health from all perspectives and all dimensions. Learning to consciously open up these levels of the subconscious will help trigger specific healing effects. It will not only directly influence various body functions, but it will also help us to awaken to an understanding of the metaphysical stimuli behind the problem. We begin by learning something about the energies of each of these levels of the subconscious mind.

Malkuth—

Basic Colors: Black, olive-green, russet, and citrine.
Astrological Influence: The Earth.
Healing Archangel: Sandalphon (San-Dahl-Fon).

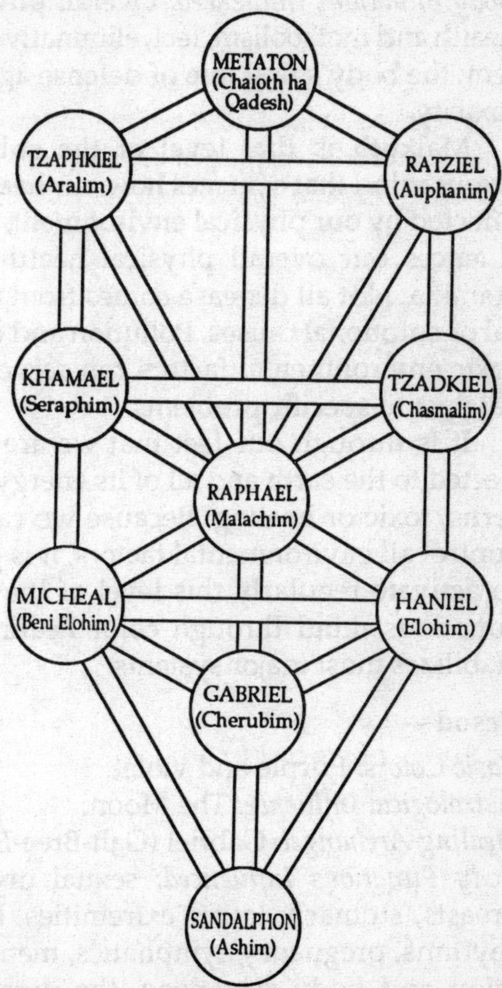

Healing Angels of the Tree of Life

Body Functions Influenced: Overall physical health and metabolism, feet, eliminative system, the body's first line of defense against toxicity.

Malkuth is that level of the subconscious mind that oversees how our health is affected by our physical environment. It influences our overall physical health and stamina. Not all dis-ease comes from mental or emotional causes. Pollution and other toxic environmental factors can serve as a catalyst to specific problems.

It is through our feet that we are connected to the earth and all of its energy patterns, toxic or healing. Because we cannot control all environmental factors, it is good to activate regularly this level of the subconscious mind through color healing. It stabilizes most major systems.

Yesod—

Basic Colors: Purple and violet.
Astrological Influence: The Moon.
Healing Archangel: Gabriel (Gah-Bree-Ehl).
Body Functions Influenced: sexual organs, breasts, stomach, lower extremities, body rhythms, pregnancy, lymphatics, menstruation and body secretions, the digestive system.

Yesod is that level of the subconscious which oversees the activities of sexual energy and sexual development. It has ties to the Eastern concept of the kundalini, the primal sacred life force. This is also the level of the subconscious that directs our body rhythms —the highs, the lows, the fluctuations we encounter on a daily and monthly cycle.

It is at this level of the subconscious that we can come to an understanding of how our emotions are affecting our overall health foundations. This is a level of the subconscious that can help us to attune more psychically to our health or the health of another.

Hod—

Basic Color: Orange.
Astrological Influence: Mercury.
Healing Archangel: Michael (Mee-Kah-Ehl).
Body Functions Influenced: Nervous system, respiratory system, lungs, hands, right hip, vocal cords (speech), memory, hearing and sight, pancreas.

Hod is that level of the subconscious mind which mediates the nervous and respiratory systems to a great degree. It has connections to the left hemisphere brain activities as well. Any kind of nervous, respiratory, and even intestinal problem can be alleviated by stimulating this level of the subconscious. It can also influence sugar-related diseases.

This is a level of the subconscious that we need to activate if we are having difficulty with communication in any form. It is a level that can facilitate receptiveness to all forms of doctoring. It is a level that can help us learn more about the functioning of our own body—its strengths and weaknesses.

Netzach—

Basic Color: Emerald.
Astrological Influence: Venus.
Healing Archangel: Haniel (Hah-Ni-Ehl).
Body Functions Influenced: All major aspects of physical appearance (skin, hair, etc.), female sex organs, reproduction, mammary glands, menstruation, throat, kidneys, the left hip area of the body, acid-alkaline balance, thyroid.

Netzach is that area of the subconscious mind that directs not only our physical appearance, but how we truly feel about it. It has ties to the kidneys and to some degree the eliminative system of the body. It influences the sex organs, especially in women, and it is a level that can be activated to ease menstrual problems, pregnancy difficulties, and any generative troubles.

Netzach is a level of the mind that is also connected to our emotional states. It can be useful to activate when physical problems are being complicated and intensified by emotional states. This level can be activated to facilitate healing through art therapy, color healings, and dance and movement therapies.

Tiphareth—

Basic Color: Yellow (Gold).
Astrological Influence: Sun.
Healing Archangel: Raphael (Rah-Fah-Ehl).
Body Function Influenced: Overall vitality, functions of the heart, the circulatory system, the immune system, the thymus gland, metabolism, spinal cord, physical growth.

Tiphareth is a powerful level of the subconscious mind, especially in the healing process. If unsure as to which level of the subconscious to stimulate for healing a condition, you cannot go wrong by stimulating this one. It affects the entire body's metabolism and balance.

This level has a direct link to the immune system of the body, and it is the heart of our physical health manifestations. The archangel associated with this level is Raphael who is known as the angel of brightness, beauty and HEALING. This level can be crucial to the turn around of many systemic problems.

Geburah—

Basic Color: Red.
Astrological Influence: Mars.
Healing Archangel: Kamael (Kah-Mah-Ehl).
Body Functions Influenced: The activities and the production of red corpuscles, the muscles of the body (voluntary and involuntary), the male sex organs, some affect upon the reproductive system, excretory organs, prostrate gland, colon.

Geburah is a level of the subconscious mind which should be activated in times of feverish conditions and with any inflammatory disease. In times of surgery and accidents, this level can stimulate greater strength and recuperative powers.

This level has ties to the blood within the body, especially the production of red corpuscles. In cases of anemia, stimulating this level can be beneficial. Infections in the blood stream can be affected through this level of the subconscious, along with deep-seated diseases.

Chesed—

Basic Color: Blue.
Astrological Influence: Jupiter.
Healing Archangel: Tzadkiel (Zahd-Ki-Ehl).
Basic Body Influences: Blood (venous activity), liver, cell nutrition, hips and thighs, buttocks, cerebral hemispheres, intestines.

Chesed is that level of the subconscious mind that mediates cell nutrition. It is a level connected to the body's ability to detoxify the blood system—one of the functions of the liver, which is ruled by Jupiter.

Problems with weight, too much or too little, can be influenced by stimulating and working with this level. This includes obesity as well as anorexia. With more and more food stuffs having less vitamin and mineral content, this is a level we need to stimulate regularly. It enables us to extract as much nutrition from what we eat as possible.

Binah—

Basic Color: Black.
Astrological Influence: Saturn.
Healing Archangel: Tzaphkiel (Zahf-Ki-Ehl).
Body Functions Influenced: Skin, bones, teeth, joints, hearing, spleen, proper functioning of tendons and cartilage, gall bladder.

Binah is a powerful center to stimulate to affect the length of time of recovery from illness. It is a dynamic center to stimulate at times of colds, chills and rheumatism. It has an affect upon congestion in the body and the ossification of the bones. It can be stimulated to ease arthritis as well.

Binah is a level of the subconscious mind that can be stimulated to either ease the transition from life to death or to override near fatal diseases, accidents, etc. Stimulating it can facilitate getting past a critical point in an illness.

Chokmah—

Basic Color: Gray.
Astrological Influence: Neptune.
Healing Archangel: Ratziel (Rah-Tzi-Ehl).
Body Functions Influenced: Pineal gland, nervous system, cones and rods of the eyes, mental illness, lymph glands, the feet, nerve synapses in the brain.

This is a level of the subconscious that strongly affects the entire lymphatic system of the body. This includes all of the glands, their functions and their connections to the chakras. It can be stimulated to ease allergic conditions and to identify their source. This level can also help us in handling contagious diseases, and it can assist us with physical problems associated with addictive behaviors (drugs, alcohol, etc.). It can be activated to ease colds and mucous conditions.

This is a level of the subconscious that can assist all psychological therapies. It is directly linked to our mental health, as it influences physical conditions. It can be awakened to reveal the metaphysical causes of physical conditions. It can enable us to see more clearly.

Kether—

Basic Color: White.
Astrological Influence: Uranus.
Healing Archangel: Metatron (Meh-Tuh-Tron).
Body Functions Influenced: Regenerative forces of the reproductive system, body oxygenation, ankles, most syndromes, electrical impulses in the cells, the nervous system, spinal cord, some aspects of vision.

This can be a very important level of the subconscious when working with our health. Activating this level can bring clarification of symptoms and problems that previously could not be identified. Many syndromes are difficult to define, but this is a level that can facilitate drawing out the right information.

This level of the subconscious can positively influence many nervous disorders and ease conditions stemming from "incurable" problems and complaints. When stimulated properly, this level can also ease glaucoma and cataracts.

Tree of Life Healing Techniques

There are many techniques for using the Tree of Life in healing work—even in color healing. As we will see in the next chapter, there are four sets of color for each level of the Tree of Life. Each of these colors activates a level of the subconscious mind in its own specific manner.

In the previous pages, we gave only one basic healing color for each level. This basic color is one which stimulates the subconscious mind in a way that opens it more effectively to the imaginative faculty, to the creative powers of the mind. It is a color that stimulates the creative energies at that level of the subconscious.

It also helps us to connect more easily through that level of the subconscious to the healing ministrations of the archangel. We can thus experience the healing energies more tangibly. This does not mean that the other colors discussed in the next chapter are ineffective. Rather, it means that the color already cited for that level is the color

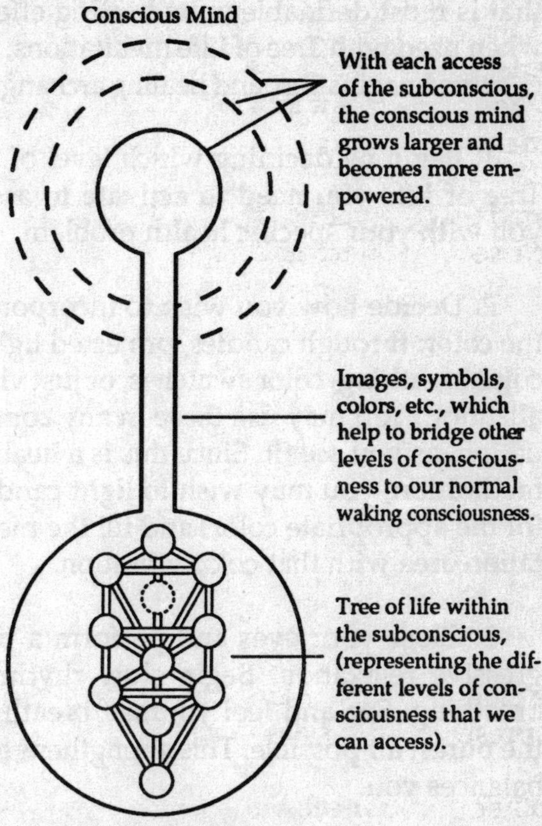
Conscious Mind
With each access of the subconscious, the conscious mind grows larger and becomes more empowered.
Images, symbols, colors, etc., which help to bridge other levels of consciousness to our normal waking consciousness.
Tree of life within the subconscious, (representing the different levels of consciousness that we can access).
Subconscious Mind

Tapping Our Hidden Levels

In the Qabala color meditation techniques, we use colors to stimulate specific levels of the subconscious mind this enables us to more effectively direct body processes and alter health factors that are controlled by that level of the mind.

that is most definable in its healing effects when used with Tree of Life meditations, the creative imagination, and healing archangels.

1. Begin by deciding which level of the Tree of Life you need to activate to assist you with your specific health problem.

2. Decide how you wish to incorporate the color: through candles, projected lights, color breathing, color swatches, or just visualization. You may use these in any combination, as you see fit. Since this is a healing meditation, you may wish to light candles (of the appropriate color) and fill the meditation area with that color vibration.

3. Close your eyes and perform a progressive relaxation. Begin slow rhythmic breathing. See and feel yourself breathing the purest air possible. This strengthens and balances you.

4. Now, as you continue breathing slowly and regularly, visualize the air you breathe in as changing to the color and vibrancy of the appropriate level in the Tree of Life. See your body and your aura filling with this color. As you do this, visualize, imagine,

and create within your own mind the scene which follows. The color you use in this meditation is one that activates the creative powers of the mind. This enhances the imaginative faculty, and facilitates the opening of the specific level of the subconscious.

5. You begin to see in your mind's eye a scene. You are standing in a meadow. The day is cloudy; grey tints the whole scene. There are flowers in the meadow, but they either are not in bloom or are drooping. They mimic how you feel on some level.

In the middle of this meadow is a large tree. Its roots extend deep into the heart of the earth itself and its upper branches are lost in the gray skies above. As large as it is, even the tree seems to droop.

You walk slowly towards it, and you see a small opening at its base. From this opening comes a soft light, the color you visualized at the beginning of this meditation. It is the color of the Tree of Life level you need to activate to help strengthen your own health.

You pause briefly and then step inside the tree. The inside is warm and comfortable. It shines with the soft color of the level you were seeking. It is comforting, and you breath deeply of the color. It relaxes and soothes.

In the center is an altar upon which burns an eternal flame, a reminder to see this place as a temple within your own mind. The flame is small and soft, flickering occasionally. You notice as you relax and absorb the color of this temple, the flame stabilizes and grows stronger. The altar is bordered by two pillars, reminders to maintain balance in your life.

In front of the altar is a soft light, hovering as if waiting to be called forth. You remember the healing archangel to whom you have access through this level of your mind. Softly, in a whisper, you speak the archangelic name syllable by syllable. The light grows stronger.

You speak the name again—this time with more confidence. The light shifts and dances and begins to take form. You are beginning to see a glowing outline of a great figure.

Yet a third time, you speak the name—toning it strongly. The light shimmers, brightens, and then crystallizes. Before you now stands a magnificent being of beauty and light. The energy radiating from this great being is like wings enveloping the entire inner temple. It touches you and lifts your heart.

The flame upon the altar grows stronger, brightening and illuminating the temple.

The colors of the temple crystallize with diamond-like brilliance.

Softly in your mind, you hear your name spoken. You raise your eyes to this wondrous archangel. The eyes hold you; you are transfixed. Those eyes are older than time, and they are filled with such strength and unconditional love!

As the eyes stare into your own eyes, images begin to fill your mind. Strange and unfamiliar at first, you soon begin to recognize your own body—from the inside! You are being shown where the problem lies and how it affects other organs and systems of the body.

You begin to hear voices—your own and those of others. You see whole scenarios being acted out and see what the repercussions are for your own body. You begin to see the emotions and mental attitudes (of yourself and others) that have contributed to your condition.

As the images fade, this archangel steps forward. The wings of energy fan the air, filling it with the brilliant colors. You are embraced and a kiss is placed upon your head. Shivers of delight run throughout your body and soul. You see and feel yourself filling with the colors of the temple. You see and feel yourself restored to perfect balance. You are filled with exquisite joy and energy.

As the great being steps back, you see the temple fill with even greater intensities of the color, a reminder to you of the infinite health and energy available to you. Gently you reach out with your heart and mind, daring to touch and thank this magnificent one. For a brief moment, you feel one with this being, and you know your health will only continue to improve, second by second, day by day from this time forth.

The archangel steps back behind the alter and begins to recede from view. With the archangel gone, the altar is again completely visible. The light upon it now shines strong and brilliant and steady. This lamp reflects your own health. As you use these inner temples to balance and strengthen yourself, the inner lamps will grow brighter and shine more strongly within you.

You breathe deeply the energy of this inner temple, feeling yourself strong and rejuvenated. You are healthy and balanced, and it is this that you carry out of the Tree of Life into the physical world.

As you step outside the Tree, you are surprised. The gray skies are gone. Sunlight fills the meadow, warming and soothing all within it. The meadow flowers are in full bloom and color. The entire meadow looks as if it has been washed with every color of the rainbow.

You turn to look back at the tree. No longer does it droop. It is strong, tall and vibrant. It is filled with new buds and bright green leaves.

You breathe in the crisp air. The image of the meadow fills your heart and your mind. You know that this is the reflection of your restored state of health. It is this which you have awakened and created and which you now bring back with you to your present surroundings. You have learned to stimulate the subconscious to create the gift of health and vibrancy.

10

COLORS OF THE FOUR WORLDS

As we have discussed, the human essence is comprised of more than just physical energies and processes. We operate on more than just a physical level. Our emotional, mental and spiritual states are intimately entwined with our physical being.

The human mind is linked to all of our dimensions. We must remember, though, that our mind is not located in the brain. Yes, there is an intimate connection between the mind and the brain, but the mind is the seat of our consciousness.

The different levels of the subconscious mind not only influence physical body functions, but they give us access to the consciousness of other planes and dimensions as well. They integrate our emotional, mental, and spiritual states into physical expression. This is why in holistic healing, the individual always looks for the metaphysical cause behind a physical problem.

Learning to work with the mind and affect it from all levels—physical, emotional, mental, and spiritual—is the key to establishing balanced health. This can be accomplished through color healing techniques—especially when utilizing a Qabalistic system of colors.

In the previous chapter we dealt with only one basic color for activating the different levels of the subconscious mind depicted in the Tree of Life. That color stimulated the imaginative faculty of the subconscious in a manner that opened us to the healing ministrations of the archangels operating around us.

There are other colors associated with each of the ten levels in the Tree of Life. Traditionally, the Tree of Life is divided into four worlds. These four worlds correspond to the physical, the emotional (astral), the mental, and the spiritual. "The Four Worlds" diagram shows one way of looking at this process. In this diagram, different levels of the subconscious give us access to different planes and energies.

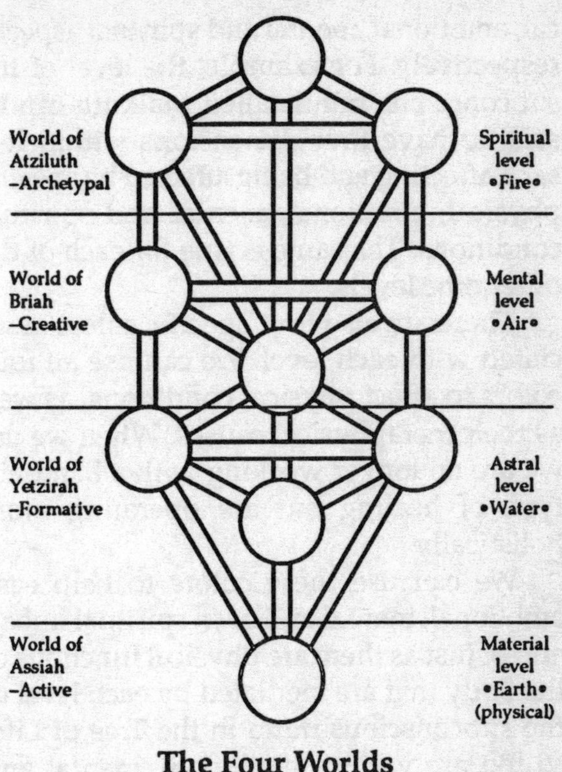

The Four Worlds

A truer depiction of how this operates can be found in "The Tree of Life in all Four Worlds" diagram. In this depiction, each of the ten levels of the subconscious mind can be seen as operating on four levels. Each has a level within it that influences physical, emotional, mental and spiritual aspects, respectively. For example, the level of the subconscious mind called Malkuth can be seen to have four dimensions within it—each affecting and being affected by specific physical, emotional, mental and spiritual conditions. The same is true for each of the other nine levels.

There are also four specific colors associated with each level. We can use all four colors to affect physical conditions, as well as their metaphysical causes. When we do, we are no longer working with a band-aid type of healing but are operating more holistically.

We can use these colors to help ease emotional, mental and even spiritual imbalances. Just as there are physical functions of the body that are mediated by each level of the subconscious mind in the Tree of Life, so too are various emotional, mental and spiritual states.

In the previous chapter we discussed the basic body functions mediated by each of the levels. There are certain non-physical states that are more likely to create an imbalance in that level of the subconscious mind, helping to manifest specific physical imbalances. In this chapter, we will explore

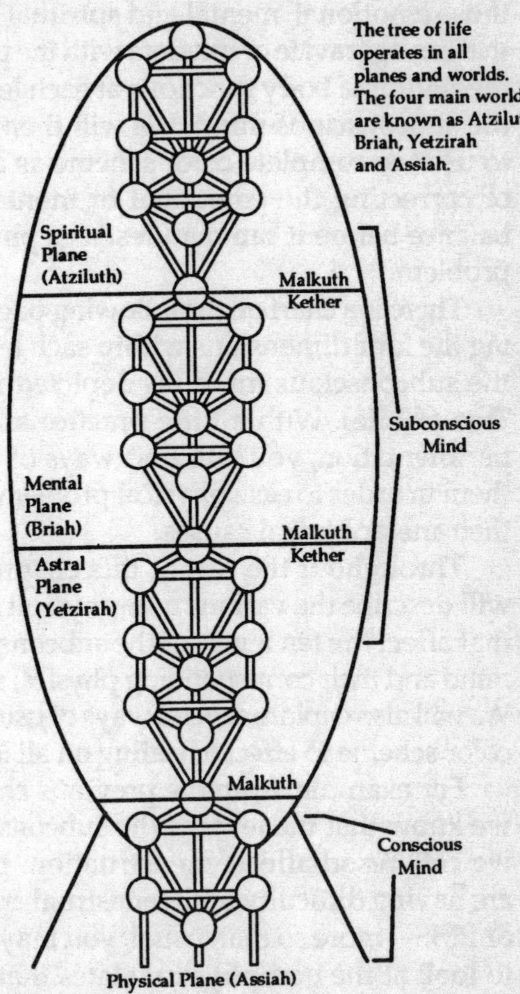

The Tree of Life in All Four Worlds

those emotional, mental and spiritual states that can aggravate or interfere with the proper mediation of body functions at each level of the subconscious mind. We will then learn to use the complete color scheme as a way of correcting the emotional or mental imbalance before it can manifest as a physical problem.

There is a chart on the following page giving the four dimensions within each level of the subconscious mind (as depicted in the Tree of Life). With a little practice and experimentation, you will find ways of using them in order to ease physical problems and their metaphysical causes.

Throughout the rest of this chapter we will describe the various non-physical states that affect the ten levels of the subconscious mind and their corresponding physical states. We will also explore several ways of using the color scheme to effect a healing on all levels.

For example, from the previous chapter we know that the level of the subconscious we call Yesod affects menstruation. If you are having difficulty with menstrual cramps or PMS—more so than usual, you may wish to look at the non-physical states that may create problems or aggravate physical conditions mediated by Yesod. Have you been

THE COLOR SCHEME OF THE FOUR WORLDS

LEVEL	SPIRITUAL	MENTAL	ASTRAL	PHYSICAL
Kether	Brilliance	White Brilliance	White Brilliance	White with Gold
Chokmah	Soft Blue	Grey	Mother of Pearl	White with Red, Blue, Yellow
Binah	Crimson	Black	Dark Brown	Grey with Pink
Chesed	Deep Violet	Blue	Deep Purple	Azure with Yellow
Geburah	Orange	Scarlet	Bright Scarlet	Red with Black
Tiphareth	Pink Rose	Yellow	Salmon	Amber
Netzach	Amber	Emerald	Yellow-Green	Olive with Gold
Hod	Violet Purple	Orange	Red Russet	Yellow-Brown
Yesod	Indigo	Violet	Dark Purple	Citrine with Azure
Malkuth	Yellow	Black, Olive Russet and Citrine	Black, Olive, Russet and Citrine with Gold flecks	Black-rayed Yellow

dealing with sexual issues recently? Have you expressed or been exposed to arrogance? Has vanity been an issue recently?

Even if you can't identify a non-physical state that may have contributed to the condition, it is a good idea to use the complete color scheme for the level. This ensures balance on all levels. (Sometimes it is easy to overlook possibilities and objectively evaluate what we have been feeling.)

The inverse is also true. If you can identify which emotions and mental attitudes (the non-physical states) you have experienced or been exposed to, it is easier to identify where a physical problem is more likely to manifest. We can then use the colors on a regular basis to prevent the determined level from becoming so out of balance that a physical problem manifests.

Malkuth—

Malkuth is adversely affected by specific non-physical states. These include laziness, greed and avarice. Recklessness, aggression, and lack of discernment can cause or reflect problems in this level of the subconscious. They can eventually lead to physical problems in areas discussed in the previous chapter. A lack of physical activity and never acting upon one's planning can also create imbalances in this level of the mind.

Yesod—

The physical body functions mediated by Yesod can also be adversely affected by non-physical states. These include idleness, any emotional stress or imbalance, problems with sexuality, and vanity. A lack of confidence and independence can reflect a need for work on this level of the mind with the whole color scheme.

Hod—

The physical functions of the body mediated by Hod can be adversely affected by deceit and dishonesty. Impatience, criticalness and aloofness can also manifest with physical problems in those body functions controlled by this level of the subconscious mind. Difficulty with speech and communication, a lack of precision, and impractical behaviors can also cause or reflect a need for some color balancing.

Netzach—

Lust and impurity, along with over-emotionalism, can create imbalances in this level of the mind, affecting the previously specified physical functions. Being exposed to possessiveness, introversion, jealousy and defeatism can reflect a need for color balancing through this level's four-fold scheme. Expressing any of those qualities can also indicated the need for color balancing at this level. Anti-social behavior and lack of emotional control can also reflect or cause imbalances.

Tiphareth—

Being exposed to or experiencing certain non-physical states can adversely affect how this level mediates physical activities of the body. Anger is very detrimental, as is insecurity and false pride. A lack of compassion and mistrust can also reflect a need for working with the entire color scheme of this level. A pessimistic view on most things will often indicate a need for healing and balancing this level of the subconscious mind.

Geburah—

This is a level that is often more easily identifiable as needing healing work. Hostility and fear often reflect imbalances and can cause physical problems in those areas of body activity mediated by Geburah. Hyperactivity, bullying, timidity and a surrendering attitude can also create problems. A lack of confidence and a lack of critical judgment can create imbalances as well, and thus require a full color scheme healing.

Chesed—

Those body functions mediated and controlled by Chesed can also be adversely affected by non-physical states. This includes self-expressions of hypocrisy, stinginess, self-righteousness, and the state of being overly conservative. An individual who is slow to respond, or is melancholy may eventually manifest imbalances in those physical areas mediated by this level. In such cases, the use of the four-fold color scheme will help restore balance.

Binah—

This level of the subconscious can also be affected by non-physical states, which in turn will affect those body functions mediated by it. Fear can be a major concern at this level, especially fear of the dark and of the future. An individual who is introverted may need to work with the whole color scheme, as well as anyone who is always sacrificing himself/herself. If there is a lack of confidentiality, a lack of nurturing, or a failure to understand and employ patience, problems can occur that can best be corrected by using the entire color scheme.

Chokmah—

As with the others, certain non-physical states can interfere with the proper functioning of this level of the subconscious mind. This in turn will affect those body functions mediated by it. Being overly superstitious or misguidedly futuristic can lend you into some problems down the road in those areas affected by this level. Constant tardiness, lateness and inefficiency can reflect some imbalances. Being forgetful and short-sighted can reflect a need to use the four-fold color scheme to eliminate these problems as well as any physical repercussions.

Kether—

A negative self-image, a lack of imagination, and an inability to initiate new things can create problems in this level of the subconscious mind. These then can show up as physical problems in those areas mediated by this level. Always seeking sympathy, easily feeling shame, feeling misunderstood, and a lack of tenderness can reflect imbalance in this level. Self-denial and becoming lost in the illusions of the imaginative world can also reflect a need to use the four-fold scheme of colors to correct and prevent physical manifestations from these.

Healing Techniques with the Four-Fold Color Scheme

Working with all four colors for each level is a little more complicated than a single color. First, it is difficult to make colored slides for some of the combinations, and it is also difficult to find candles of the appropriate colors and combinations. This should not prevent you from attempting to work with the entire color scheme for each level, as it has a powerful healing effect.

In all four of the methods discussed below, it is most effective to begin by working with the color(s) associated with the physical. Then move to the astral, then the mental, and end with the spiritual. (Refer to the chart on page 165.)

Examine the physical symptoms you are experiencing, and using the information given in this chapter and the last, determine which level(s) of the Tree of Life you need to stimulate with color. Once this is decided, simply choose one of the following techniques:

Breathing the Four Dimensions—

One of the best ways of working on yourself is through the technique of color breathing. Once you decide which level of the subconscious you need to stimulate, use the chart given earlier and determine the four colors that will effect a healing on all dimensions.

Spend three to five minutes breathing each color in, visualizing the conditions stabilizing and being healed. Start with the physical dimension and move to the astral, then do the mental, and end with the spiritual.

Simple Color Projection—

We learned earlier that we can project color through our hands at whatever frequency we are mentally focused upon. This technique is especially effective when working on someone else.

Have the person sit with their back to you with eyes closed, relaxing. Place your hands 2-3 inches above the crown of the head. If you wish, you may find it more comfortable to rest your hands directly on his/her head.

Relax yourself and begin rhythmic breathing. As you breathe in, feel the energy drawing into your body through the top of your own head. See and feel the energy in the color associated with the physical level. Feel it moving toward your hands to be projected outward.

Continue your rhythmic breathing. As you exhale, see and feel this colored energy pouring out your hands through the crown of the individual's head. See it filling the body. See it balancing, soothing and healing the specific condition, while strengthening that level of the person's subconscious mind. Continue for three to five minutes or until you feel comfortable with it.

Now pull your hands away and shake them briefly to clear the energy field. As you resume your rhythmic breathing, you see and feel yourself filling with the colored energy of the astral level. See and feel yourself pouring forth this energy to fill the being and essence of the other individual.

Repeat this procedure for the color(s) of the mental and the spiritual aspects as well. You have touched all four dimensions within that particular level of the subconscious mind. Your work has been holistic, treating physical and the metaphysical imbalances.

Candle Healing on All Dimensions—

We can adapt the techniques of candle healing to the Qabala. It takes a little more effort to find the variety of colored candles needed. You may not find candles comprised of more than one color, as is often necessary for the physical dimension of a level.

It can be just as effective to use the predominant color. A little creativity and flexibility will go a long way and does not diminish the healing effects. For example, on the physical dimension of the subconscious level of Malkuth, the color is a black-rayed yellow. Using just a yellow candle, (since it is the predominant color) is still effective.

After gathering the candles, sit or lie down on the floor. Put the candle with the color for the physical dimension in front of you, and the candle for the spiritual dimension behind you. On one side of you place the astral color candle and on the other side, the mental color candle.

Begin by lighting just the physical candle. See and feel its energy illuminating the area and being absorbed by the body, restoring balance. Next light the astral, and see and feel the emotional causes and effects of the illness being balanced. Then light the mental candle and imagine the mental attitudes that facilitated the problem being resolved and healed. Finally, light the spiritual dimension candle for the level you are working on. See it strengthening the effects of the others, and stabilizing your entire energy system.

Focus on each candle for three to five minutes. This is a powerful healing technique, and rarely takes more than three such treatments for a noticeable effect to be experienced. Wait at least 12 hours before repeating.

Awakening the Tree of Life—

This technique takes a little longer to actually perform. You can do it for yourself through visualization and rhythmic breathing. It can also be performed on another person. It should not be attempted until you have learned to perform extended periods of rhythmic breathing, as it can tend to make you hyperventilate.

Have the individual lie down, face up. Begin your own rhythmic breathing to build the energy. Begin by placing your hands at the crown of the head. This is Kether, the top of the Tree of Life. See and feel the energy pouring through your hands into this area of the body. Begin with the color for the physical dimension, and then move to the astral, mental and spiritual.

When you have done all the colors for Kether, move your hands down to the left side of the face, and begin sending the colors for Chokmah. Then do the same for Binah and all of the others, down to the feet (Malkuth). See the diagram, "Awakening the Tree of Life."

This path draws energy all through the body, while activating all levels of the subconscious mind. It takes a little longer to perform, but it is very catalytic in effecting healing changes.

A beneficial variation of this is to make four passes from top to bottom along this so-called "Path of the Flaming Sword." Begin by using all of the physical dimension colors for each level. Then start back at the top and go through all of the astral colors, followed by the mental and spiritual colors. Do the same for each level.

You will see and feel a noticeable difference when working on someone in this manner. Your energy will build. While you are helping to build and balance the other person's energies, you are also building and

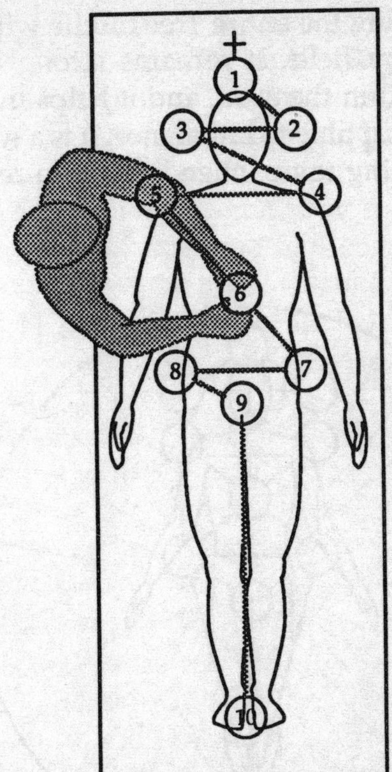

Awakening the Tree of Life

By sending energy along the ancient "Path of the Flaming Sword",* you activate a powerfully creative force. You draw it down through the body, affecting all systems and all levels of energy

*For more information on the Path of the Flaming Sword, consult the author's earlier works on the Qabala, *Simplified Magic* and *Imagick.*

strengthening the entire Tree of Life within your energy field. It remains strong and vibrant within the aura, and it helps make us less susceptible to imbalance. It is a wonderful healing tonic when used on a regular basis.

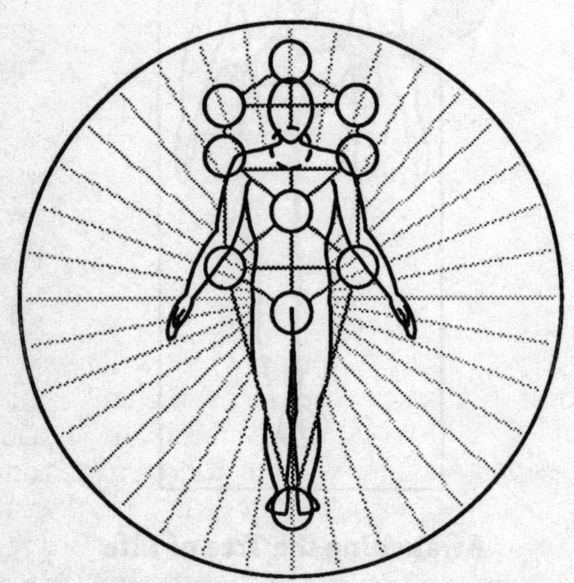

The Tree of Life Within the Aura

When the Tree of Life is built into the aura through healing, the aura begins to shine with new color, clarity and vibrancy.

11

COLOR HEALING MANDALAS

Color has been used in many ways throughout the history of humanity to express, to heal, and to illumine. It was an essential aspect of sacred art. Sacred art used color to create designs that would expand consciousness. It was believed that colors stimulated the outer eyes in a manner that awakened the inner eyes.

The mandala is the most commonly known form of sacred art. It is a tool for focusing the mind. A mandala holds the essence of a specific thought or concept. Through its design and color scheme, it draws the consciousness more fully into that concept. It creates unity. Because disease or illness reflects a breakdown in the holistic unity of the body, the mandala can be a powerful tool for color healing.

In Eastern philosophy, mandalas are commonly known as yantras. They are known as medicine shields in the native American tradition. They can be a melange of geometric patterns, colors and designs to elicit specific effects. For our purposes, we will use the term mandala to include all of its forms.

Mandalas stimulate the inner creative forces in a manner peculiar to their design. They can be constructed to arouse any inner force or desire. They are symbols for integration and transformation, a form of action and interaction with ourselves.

Mandalas serve to stimulate the primal inner sources imprinted within the deeper levels of the mind—including the inner source of our own healing. They are psychic transformers, helping us to connect with our missing parts.

Healing mandalas are designs with symbols and colors that are used to create shifts in our energy on physical and/or subtle levels. All colors, all symbols and all geometric shapes alter our electromagnetic field. In chapter eight we discussed how certain geometric shapes can be used in candle layouts to amplify and effect healing. In meditating with and constructing mandalas, we are doing the same thing.

All healing mandalas work best when made personally. The more you know about what their various symbols represent, the more receptive you will be to their influence. Constructing and coloring a mandala is itself an act of healing. It is an act of taking charge, of participating in the responsibility for your own health. The essence of art therapy has ties to this ancient concept of sacred art.

There are many methods of creating healing mandalas. This book is not the forum for exploring all of the intricacies. Instead, we will focus on some simple mandala designs that you can use to begin to have an impact upon your own health. Do not limit yourself strictly to the symbols and designs given in the rest of this chapter. They are merely guidelines, so you will have a starting point in creating your own healing art.

Creating a Color Wheel

A color wheel is a tool that helps you to be more sensitive to colors and their healing aspects. Because you are working with the full spectrum of colors, you are able to balance and heal yourself just by constructing it. Creating a color wheel for yourself is simple:

1. Draw a circle about six to seven inches in diameter.

2. Using a protractor, mark off a point every 30 degrees, and then and divide the circle into 12 equal parts. (You do not have to limit yourself to 12. You can make it four or seven or however many you wish.)

3. Then, using colored pencils, paints, or markers, color in each section. Start with red and then move through the shades to violet. You used to enjoy coloring as a child; do so again.

4. Notice how you feel as you color each section. Do you feel more drawn to some colors and not others? How does each color look when you place another color next to it? Do some of the colors make you feel better than others? Do you enjoy coloring with some shades more than others? All of these questions can provide clues to which colors are beneficial to your present health state.

5. Now create another color wheel, but change the arc that serves as each section's outer perimeter. Make it diamond-shaped, or, make it bulbous. How does this change the way you feel about the colors as you fill in the wheel?

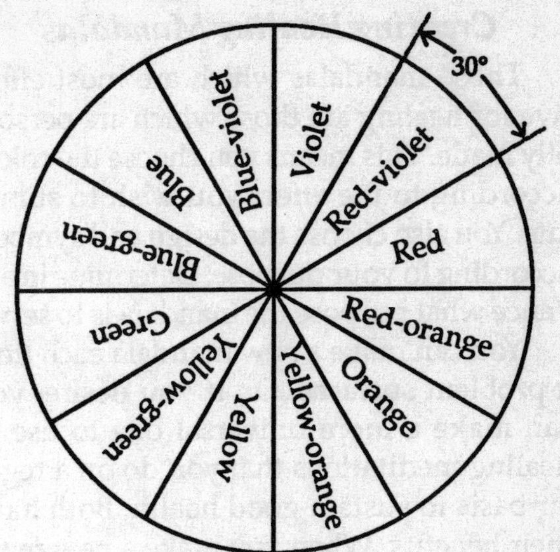

Basic Color Wheel

Augmented Color Wheel

Creating Color Wheels and Variations

Creating Healing Mandalas

Those mandalas which are most effective for healing are those which are personally made. This means you choose the colors according to the effect you wish to stimulate. You also choose the design and symbols according to your purpose. Determine in advance what purpose the mandala is to serve.

You can make a new mandala each time a problem surfaces. Or, if you desire, you can make a more universal one to use in healing meditations that you do on a regular basis to sustain good health. Both have their benefits. When you make a new mandala each time, it keeps you involved in a creative and joyful act, which in itself is healing. Mandalas that are used over extended periods of time develop a thought form of healing around them, so that their effects become stronger each time they are employed.

Whichever way you decide, make sure you keep in mind the mandala's purpose as you construct it. The more significance you attach to the colors, symbols and designs, the more they will be able to work for you.

Mandalas can be made from almost any material. Simple poster board is inexpensive and easy to work with. Be sure to make it large enough so that you can see all aspects of it when it is across the room from you.

Healing mandalas are very effective when constructed within a circular shape. We can use other geometric forms inside of that circle, but the circle is a good symbol of wholeness and unity, which is what you are trying to achieve with the healing.

Review the effects of the geometric shapes as discussed in chapter eight. Examine some of the other healing mandala forms and the effects they elicit, as given in the following pages. Choose the symbols and shapes that you need and that will activate the energies you desire through the mandala.

Then, experiment with various layouts within the circumference of your mandala circle. Try and make the layout as meaningful as possible. A dozen different people may use the same symbols and even the same colors, but the way they will be placed in the mandala will vary from individual to individual. This is as it should be.

For an example of a general healing mandala, refer to the illustration "A Healing Mandala," on the next page. It uses the symbols and shapes given in this book. It is strengthening and stabilizing to the entire metabolism of the body. It is also beneficial to the immune system, having a dynamic effect upon the heart chakra. Its effectiveness is enhanced when opposite colors are used. (Refer to the "Opposite Colors Chart" on page 56.)

The color in the mandala can also be

A Healing Mandala

This simple healing mandala uses only three symbols: the circle, an elongated six-rayed star, and the bindhu. It stabilizes and activates the heart chakra. It draws the meditator into it—into a new state of balance.

Alphabet Color Correspondences

Letters	Color(s)
A	White
B	Yellow
C	Red-Orange
D	Emerald
E	Blue
F	Light Red-Orange
G	Deep Blue
H	Bright Reds
I	Red-Violet
J	Yellow-Green
K	Blue-Violet
L	Emerald
M	Mother of Pearl
N	Blue-Green
O	Black
P	Scarlet
Q	Violet
R	Orange Amber
S	Blue
T	Green-Yellow
U	Earth Tones
V	Red Orange
W	Green Silver
X	Deep Indigo
Y	Light Golden Brown
Z	Pastel Orange

Healing Mandala Symbols

● —The bindhu, the point within the center; the supreme center of consciousness.

+ —An interaction of balance between the male and female; stabilizes the electromagnetics of the body; balance of the four elements and the four dimensions (physical, emotional, mental and spiritual).

—Activating and stimulating; releasing and freeing; the creative force.

—Equilibrium that is static and stabilized; affects the heart chakra and body metabolism.

—Equilibrium that is more dynamic; stimulating to the heart center and the immune system.

□ —Stabilizing; static; a solid, grounding foundation; affects the root chakra.

△ —Stimulating and amplifying; activates electrical aspects; fiery and masculine in nature.

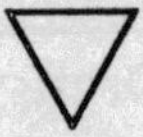

▽ —Grounding; activates the magnetic aspects of the body; watery and feminine in nature.

Egyptian Symbols of Healing

—Symbol of Isis; can be used for all female issues of health and to assist children.

—The eye of Horus; beneficial for all physical healing; preventative medicine.

—The sistrum; a symbol for Bast and beneficial for identifying the mental causes of physical illness; beneficial to mental health.

—The caduceus, a symbol for Thoth; this is the symbol for amplifying any and all of the healing arts; in meditation it helps determine the karma of disease.

—The symbol for Sirius; activates strength and stamina, opens the unconscious to healing energy.

—Hieroglyphs for life, health and prosperity.

—The Ankh; the symbol of the life force; gently strengthens the healing energies.

Other traditions have their own symbols which can be used in healing mandalas. This is but one example of a set of healing symbols. A little study of other traditions will reveal much about their healing symbols.

made more personal to you through some simple correspondences. You can use the colors associated with major aspects of your astrological chart. (The three most important aspects are your sun sign, your moon sign, and your rising sign. The colors for these three help to restore your basic energy pattern.)

Your name is also a powerful energy signature. The various elements in your name (the vowels and consonants) have specific colors associated with them. These colors are symbolic of specific energies that you have chosen on some other level to work with. They are also very healing and stabilizing to your overall energy system, physical and otherwise. Using the chart on the next page, you can incorporate your name's colors into your mandala, amplifying the effects of the mandala for you.

Healing Mandala Meditation

When you reach a point in constructing your mandala where you are unsure what to add next, stop. You have probably created what is appropriate for you at this time.

When you have finished with it, set it across from you about four to five feet away. Just sit and gaze at it for about 10 to

15 minutes. Feel its energies. Visualize everything it will do for you. Review its meanings. Ask yourself questions as you gaze upon it. Does it need other colors? Do you find it peaceful and calming? Energizing?

Try to imagine the energy flowing off from it in healing waves to surround and embrace you. Close your eyes, visualizing it within your mind. As you sit across from it with your eyes closed, what part of your body feels it most strongly?

As you sit across from it, relaxing, see it floating off of the board in waves of energy to overlay your body. See yourself in the middle of the mandala, absorbing it into your own body. Visualize this mandala shining with strength and vibrancy within you. Feel it encompassing your entire aura with healing energies. Know that each time you look upon it, or picture it in your mind, it will automatically begin to work for you.

As you work with the mandalas and all of the techniques outlined in this book, you will begin to see colors from an entirely different perspective. Each time you see any color, you will recognize that it truly is a luminescent energy. You will begin to see it as an outward reflection of the light within.

12

HOLISTIC HEALTH

Anyone can heal. Anyone can learn to administer energies that accelerate and facilitate the healing process. This can be done physically, emotionally, mentally and spiritually. The human essence is a wondrous thing. Its capacity to rejuvenate and regenerate itself is limited solely by our awareness. The amount of healing energy available to each of us is limited solely by our capacity to give love and respect everyday to ourselves and others.

Many methods of healing and doctoring exist. Everyone that you speak to has a different opinion as to which is best. The truth is that the best one is the one that works for you. Each of us has a unique energy system, and to generalize and lump all symptoms and all problems (and their respective cures) into one category does a great disservice to us as individuals and to humanity as a whole.

Part of our responsibility as an individual human being is to find that method or combination of methods that works best for us as individuals. This involves time and study, something many are not willing to do in our present society. It is amazing how ignorant most people are concerning their own physical bodies, its organs and systemic functions. There is a tendency to relegate the responsibility for our bodies and the knowledge of them to outside individuals.

Above the portals of the ancient mystery temples—the centers of higher learning, healing and spirituality—were but two words: "KNOW THYSELF!" A simple enough axiom, it is one that creates tremendous difficulty for many. People are unwilling to take the time to know themselves, thus they give that responsibility over to others. They hire individuals to "know" for them.

All healing comes from within. The body —physical and otherwise—has a tremendous capacity for restoring itself to health. Yes, because of genetics and such influences as karma, there can be a greater predisposition or preconditioning to various problems. Traditional medicine and doctoring may serve as a catalyst to correct the problem, but it often does not correct the cause of the problem. Modern medicine is still unsure how various diseases manifest. Why do they affect some people and not others? What makes some individuals prone to illness and other problems? Words such as virus, bacteria, weakened constitution, etc. are not really explanations. Viruses and bacteria surround us all the time, so why are we sick sometimes and not others?

This book is not a manual to replace orthodox medicine. The methods in here are not prescriptive. They are simply descriptions of energy applications that have been tried and found to have elicited results when used by others in the past. These healing methods have been employed in combination with orthodox medical treatments, or alone.

All treatments, orthodox and otherwise, have their function and viability. There are times when the orthodox medical approach (including surgery) is very necessary in the restoration of balance and health, but to make it exclusive as a treatment is to deny that you have any control or responsibility in your own health maintenance.

If nothing else, this manual should provide an opportunity to experience the innate subtleties of the human essence and to experience the healing ability that resides within each of us without exception. We each can assist with the healing of our bodies and our lives by expanding our perceptions and increasing our knowledge and our personal responsibility.

Working with alternative and holistic healing traditions serves many functions. It opens our awareness of how we operate on more than just a physical level. It demonstrates tangibly and visibly that we can effect changes in conditions through proper techniques. It shows us what we need to learn about ourselves, what we need to change about ourselves, and what we can control in ourselves.

Once experienced, our lives can never be the same. Everything in the world takes on greater significance. Every thought, word, and deed takes on a new importance as the interplay between your words and the physical body is understood and experienced. You begin to know that you can control much of what you experience in the line of dis-ease and ill health. You always have options. You become more aware of life and energy operating on all planes and dimensions within us and around us. You become aware that all is truly possible.

Part of what we must learn is that there is a divine spark within us. We are here in the physical to learn that life is supposed to go right. We are here to learn how to make it right. People receive answers to their prayers, experience a healing, and they exclaim, "The most AMAZING thing happened!" The truth is, prayers are supposed to be answered. Miracles are supposed to happen. Healings are supposed to occur! The AMAZING thing would be if they did not.

When we were children, we had no limits. Everything was possible. We all need to see the world sparkle again, as if for the first time. There is still adventure, health, joy and magic yet to be born within our lives. It is my hope that you experience through the techniques of this book a rebirth of the light and color within your own life, and that in turn you become a light unto others.

BIBLIOGRAPHY

Buckland, Raymond. *Practical Candleburning Rituals*. St. Paul, MN: Llewellyn Publications, 1982.

__________. *Practical Color Magic*. St. Paul, MN: Llewellyn Publications, 1984.

Cosimano, Charles. *Psionics 101*. St. Paul, MN: Llewellyn Publications, 1987.

Crookall, Robert. *Psychic Breathing*. Hollywood, CA: Newcastle Publishing, 1985.

Judith, Anodea. *Wheels of Life*. St. Paul, MN: Llewellyn Publications, 1988.

Krieger, Dolores. *The Therapeutic Touch*. Englewood Cliffs, NJ: Prentice-Hall, 1976.

MacIvor, Virginia and LaForest, Sandra. *Vibrations*. York Beach, ME: Samuel Weiser, 1979.

Nielsen, Greg and Polanski, Joseph. *Pendulum Power*. New York: Warner Destiny Books, 1977.

Ouseley, S.G.J. *Colour Meditations*. Essex, England: L.N.Fowler and Co., Ltd., 1944.

Ramacharaka, Yogi. *Science of Breath*. Chicago: Yogi Publishing Society, 1905.

Schwarz, Jack. *Human Energy Systems*. New York: E.P. Dutton, 1980.

Vinci, Leo. *Candle Magic*. Northamptonshire: Aquarian Press, 1983.

Wilson, Annie and Bek, Lilla. *What Colour Are You?* Northamptonshire: Turnstone Press, 1982.

Zi, Nancy. *The Art of Breathing*. New York: Bantam Books, 1986.

CRYSTAL BALLS & CRYSTAL BOWLS
Tools for Ancient Scrying & Modern Seership
Ted Andrews

Despite the popular use around the world of the traditional quartz crystal ball and the modern crystal bowl as magical tools, there has been little practical information on their applications and use—until now. *Crystal Balls and Crystal Bowls* takes the ancient processes of divination and scrying out of the realm of the supernatural and places them in the domain of natural knowledge.

This book reveals why crystal balls and crystal bowls are dynamic instruments for transformation, and how they can be used to divine the future, astral project, to connect with spirits, to heal and to balance the human energy system. This book explores their many functions, and reveals the secrets of vibrational energy, as well as its application for increasing intuition and activating creativity. Step-by-step, you will learn techniques for crystal gazing, scrying, attuning to spirit guides, developing clairvoyance, healing and more.

1-56718-026-4, 6 x 9, 256 pp., illus., photos $12.95

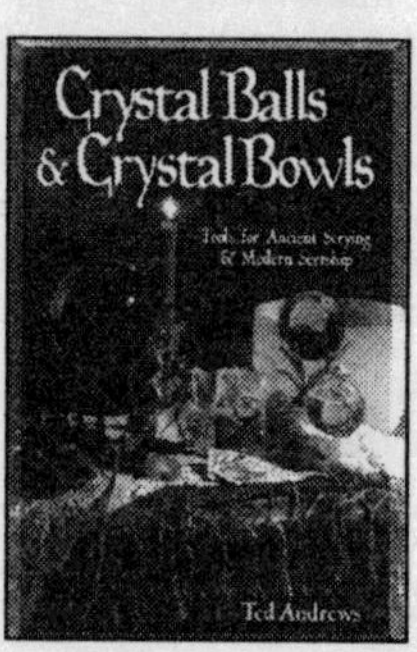

SIMPLIFIED MAGIC
A Beginner's Guide to the New Age Qabala
Ted Andrews

The qualities essential for accelerating growth and spiritual evolution are innate, but even those who recognize such potentials need an effective means of releasing them. The ancient and mystical Qabala is that means. A person does not need to become a dedicated Qabalist in order to acquire benefits from the Qabala. *Simplified Magic* offers a simple understanding of what the Qabala is and how it operates.

The Qabala is more than just some theory for ceremonial magicians. It is a system for personal attainment and magic that anyone can learn and put to use in his or her life. The secret is that the main glyph of the Qabala, the Tree of Life, is within you. The Tree of Life is a map to the levels of consciousness, power and magic that are contained within. By learning the Qabala, you will be able to tap into these levels and bring peace, healing, power, love, light and magic into your life.

0-87542-015-X, 208 pp., mass market, illus. $4.99

HOW TO MEET & WORK WITH SPIRIT GUIDES
Ted Andrews

We often experience spirit contact in our lives but fail to recognize it. Now you can learn to access and attune to beings such as guardian angels, nature spirits and elementals, spirit totems, archangels, gods and goddesses—as well as family and friends after their physical death.

Contact with higher soul energies strengthens the will and enlightens the mind. Through a series of simple exercises, you can safely and gradually increase your awareness of spirits and your ability to identify them. You will learn to develop an intentional and directed contact with any number of spirit beings. Discover meditations to open up your subconscious. Read *How to Meet and Work with Spirit Guides* and take your first steps through the corridors of life beyond the physical.

0–87542–008–7, 192 pp., mass market, illus. $4.99

ENCHANTMENT OF THE FAERIE REALM
Communicate with Nature Spirits & Elementals
Ted Andrews

Nothing fires the imagination more than the idea of faeries and elves. Folklore research reveals that people from all over the world believe in rare creatures and magickal realms. Unfortunately, in our search for the modern life we have grown insensitive to the nuances of nature. Yet those ancient realms do still exist, though the doorways to them are more obscure.

Enchantment of the Faerie Realm will help you to remember and realize that faeries and elves still dance in nature and in your heart. With just a little patience, persistence and instruction, you will learn how to recognize the presence of faeries, nature spirits, devas, elves and elementals. You will learn which you can connect with most easily. You will discover the best times and places for faerie approach. By opening to the hidden realms of life and their resources, you open your innate ability to work with energy and life at all levels.

0-87542-002-8, 240 pp., 6 x 9, illus., softcover $10.00

THE OCCULT CHRIST

Angelic Mysteries • Seasonal Rituals • The Divine Feminine

Ted Andrews

Few people realize that great mystical secrets lie hidden within the teachings of Christianity—secrets to the laws of the universe and their application in our lives. *The Occult Christ* reveals this hidden wisdom and knowledge within Biblical Scripture and presents Christianity as a Modern Mystery School in the manner of the ancient traditions throughout the world.

Within the Christ Mysteries is the cosmic effort to restore the experience of mysticism, power and the Divine on a personal level. This path not only acknowledges the Divine Feminine within the Universe and the individual, but it also reveals the means to unfold it within your life. You are shown how to access great universal and Divine power through the sacred festivals of the changing of the seasons—times in which the veil between the physical and the spiritual is thinnest. The true Christ Mysteries open the angelic hierarchies to humanity and shows the way to attune to them for greater self-knowledge, self-mastery and self-realization.

0-87542-019-2, 224 pp., 6 x 9, softcover **$12.95**

To order, call 1–800–THE MOON
Prices subject to change without notice

HOW TO UNCOVER YOUR PAST LIVES
Ted Andrews

Knowledge of your past lives can be extremely rewarding. It can assist you in opening to new depths within your own psychological makeup. It can provide greater insight into present circumstances with loved ones, career and health. It is also a lot of fun. To explore your past lives, you need only use one or more of the techniques offered. Complete instructions are provided for a safe and easy regression. Learn to dowse to pinpoint the years and places of your lives with great accuracy, make your own self-hypnosis tape, attune to the incoming child during pregnancy, use the tarot and the cabala in past life meditations, keep a past life journal and more.

0-87542-022-2, 240 pp., mass market, illus. $4.99

HOW TO DEVELOP & USE PSYCHIC TOUCH
Ted Andrews

What if a chair could speak? What if you could pick up a pen and tell what kind of day its owner had had? What if you could touch someone and know what kind of person he or she truly was—or sense pain or illness? These examples just scratch the surface of the applications of psychometry: the ability to read the psychic imprints that exist upon objects, people and places.

Everyone is psychic. Unfortunately, most of the time we brush aside our psychic impressions. Now, everyone can learn to develop their own natural sensitivities. *How to Develop and Use Psychic Touch* will teach you to assess your own abilities and provide you with a step-by-step process for developing your natural psychic abilities, including over twenty-five exercises to heighten your normal sense of touch to new levels of sensitivity.

1-56718-027-2, mass market, 224 pp., illus. $3.99

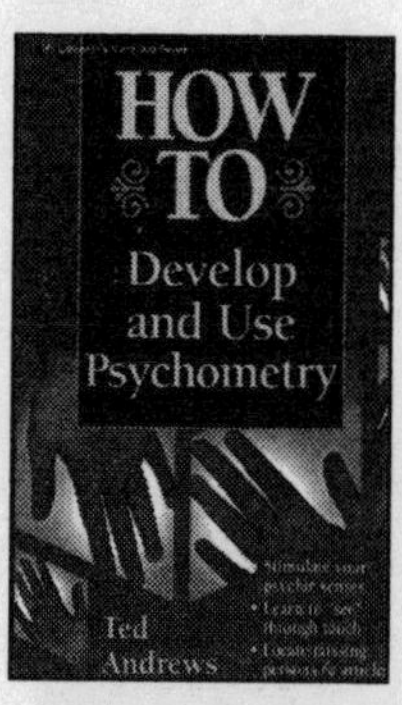

To order, call 1–800–THE MOON
Prices subject to change without notice

ANIMAL-SPEAK
The Spiritual & Magical Powers of Creatures Great & Small
Ted Andrews

The animal world has much to teach us. Some are experts at survival and adaptation, some never get cancer, some embody strength and courage while others exude playfulness. Animals remind us of the potential we can unfold, but before we can learn from them, we must first be able to speak with them.

In Animal-Speak, myth as well as fact are combined in a manner that will teach you how to speak and understand the language of the animals in your life. Animal-Speak helps you meet and work with animals as totems and spirits—by learning the language of their behaviors within the physical world. It provides techniques for reading signs and omens in nature so you can open to higher perceptions and even prophecy. It reveals the hidden, mythical and realistic roles of 45 animals, 60 birds, eight insects, and six reptiles.

Animals will become a part of you, revealing to you the majesty and divine in all life. They will restore your childlike wonder of the world and strengthen your belief in magic, dreams and possibilities.

0–87542–028–1, 400 pp., 7 x 10, illus., softcover $17.95

To order, call 1–800–THE MOON
Prices subject to change without notice